ADULTS
WITH LEARNING DIFFICULTIES

WITHDRAWN

Self Advocacy and Adults with Learning Difficulties

Contexts and Debates

Jeannie Sutcliffe and Ken Simons

National Institute of Adult Continuing Education

*First published in 1993 by the National Institute of
Adult Continuing Education (England and Wales)
21 De Montfort Street, Leicester LE1 7GE.*

*Company no. 2603322
Charity No. 1002775*

© *NIACE 1993
Reprinted 1995*

British Library Cataloguing in Publication Data
*A CIP record for this book is available from the
British Library*

ISBN 1 872941 27 3

*The Joseph Rowntree Foundation has supported this
project as part of its programme of research and innovative
development projects, which it hopes will be of value to
policy makers and practitioners. The facts presented and
views expressed in this publication, however, are those of
the authors and not necessarily those of the Foundation.*

Cover design by Paul Vann

*Printed and bound in Great Britain by Antony
Rowe Ltd., Chippenham, Wilts.*

Contents

Introduction

About the book

This publication addresses some of the issues and dilemmas related to developing self advocacy for and with adults with learning difficulties. It brings together the work of two Joseph Rowntree Foundation-funded projects. The Bristol Advocacy Project has provided an opportunity for an in-depth exploration of three self advocacy groups, where 110 people, 79 of them with learning difficulties, were interviewed about their experiences of self advocacy. The NIACE project has highlighted good practice in continuing education for adults with learning difficulties. People on the NIACE network active in self advocacy all over England and Wales were invited to share their perspectives.

Who is it for?

The book is aimed at people working to support the development of self advocacy in a range of settings. This includes: advisers to self advocacy groups, tutors of self advocacy courses and staff working to promote self advocacy in education, social services, health, private or voluntary organisations. A separate version of the Bristol Advocacy Project findings has been produced in a format designed to be accessible for adults with learning difficulties.

What are the messages?

There are three key themes which recur throughout the book:

Self advocacy is complex and diverse. There are many forms of self advocacy operating in all sorts of contexts. This diversity is a strength, offering a range of opportunities for people to become involved. There is no 'right' kind of self advocacy, although there are plenty of pitfalls. Self advocacy is complex; it raises a multitude of issues and dilemmas for everyone involved.

Self advocacy takes time. The pace of self advocacy cannot be forced. Individuals and groups need time to develop at their own speed. This frequently takes longer than professionals and supporters anticipate.

Self advocacy needs resources. Self advocacy groups and those putting on courses have to meet expenses for books, materials, room hire, transport, office costs, conferences and course fees. Securing funds while remaining independent from service providers poses a continual difficulty.

Further information about the two projects

The NIACE project has set out to document good practice in continuing education for adults with learning difficulties across agencies. Self advocacy was highlighted as an area of particular interest by practitioners on the project network, many of whom are working towards developments in their local areas. This publication is the second in a series of three practitioner-oriented books focusing on issues arising from the original project handbook by Jeannie Sutcliffe, *Adults with Learning Difficulties: Education for choice and empowerment* (NIACE and the Open University Press, 1990). For further information and related publications, contact:

NIACE
19B De Montfort Street
LEICESTER LE1 7GE

The Bristol Advocacy Project has looked at the experiences of people with learning difficulties involved in the self advocacy and the citizen advocacy movements. For a full publications list, contact:

The Bristol Advocacy Project
The Norah Fry Research Centre
32 Tyndall's Park Road
BRISTOL BS8 1PY

Chapter 1

Definitions and Diversity

There are many different kinds of self advocacy. The examples in this chapter offer insights into the forms self advocacy can take and illustrate the ways in which groups and courses operate.

This chapter attempts to bring together definitions of self advocacy and to illustrate the diversity of self advocacy that is developing. Within this range, there are crucial differences in the way that self advocacy is organised and what it means to those involved. Groups and courses have been established in day centres, hospitals, adult education centres and in community-based settings. Some groups are fully independent, while others are service-based.

Definitions

Defining self advocacy is difficult but important. As one person observed: 'It can mean so many things to so many people!' One adviser commented: 'When I first got involved in self advocacy some years ago, I felt that I had a clear idea what it was about. Now it feels much more complex, and I find it increasingly difficult to answer the question "What is self advocacy?"' The following definitions by adults with learning difficulties from Somerset and from a group of professionals indicate the diverse and subtle range of interpretations which the words 'self advocacy' can convey.

How adults with learning difficulties see self advocacy

- a voice for everyone
- making things happen
- speaking up for yourself
- company
- making our own choices
- being with people
- helping those who need more help
- looking after yourself
- having a voice of your own
- coming to the meeting
- making yourself known
- being listened to
- self confidence
- equal rights

2

- people and meetings
- friends and friendship

(List compiled by People First of Yeovil and guests from Frome, April 1990.)

How staff see self advocacy

In a workshop about self advocacy held in February 1992 for staff in Leicestershire, people came up with the following definitions:

- rights and choice
- choice, opportunity, control
- to speak, put into words
- stating a case
- independence and autonomy
- putting forward someone else's view
- speaking up, representing others, influencing others.

The term self advocacy

It is clear that there are many individual variations in the meaning which people give to the words 'self advocacy'. Some professionals are uncomfortable with the term. According to one residential worker: 'Self advocacy is an agency term for people who want to speak for themselves.' However, many adults with learning difficulties do readily use the term. Nick Rowe from Skills for People says: 'We're struggling with the issues.' The latest courses developed by people with disabilities at Skills for People do not use the term 'self advocacy' but instead are described as 'Speaking up for yourself' or 'Saying what you like or don't like'. Some groups prefer to use 'talking together' rather than 'self advocacy' to describe their activities. However, the term self advocacy has been widely adopted and is used in this publication.

Models of self advocacy

Individual

People speaking up and taking action as individuals. Many adults with learning difficulties will have been through experiences that have literally disempowered them as individuals, leaving them passive and reluctant to express an opinion or make choices. In this context self advocacy is about a process of self-development; people becoming confident and assertive enough to put forward their views about their lives. This can range from small choices, such as what to eat or what to wear, to major life decisions on where to live or whether to get a job.

Collective
People forming groups to discuss things and to try and change things collectively. A self advocacy group is run by people with learning difficulties and not by professionals. This definition embraces various forms making up the self advocacy movement, for example discussion groups based in adult or further education; service-based groups in day centres, hostels or hospitals. These might be:

- elected committees (some areas have a policy that all day centres should have an elected committee)
- users' groups open to all
- independent groups. These are based outside services, and are often (but not always) called People First groups. People First groups throughout the country are becoming increasingly influential, organising conferences and workshops, and taking part in staff training. Many act as pressure groups, working to make the views of their members heard.

Some self advocacy organisations defy categorisation. For example, Advocacy In Action in Nottingham operates as a collective in which people with and without disabilities work jointly together. Given the diversity of self advocacy, to impose a formal definition would be limiting. Rather, it is important to reflect on the questions:

- how does a self advocacy group differ from other groups for adults with learning difficulties?
- what are the boundaries?
- where does self advocacy begin?

The distinguishing feature of self advocacy is that it is a

process and also a movement controlled by adults with learning difficulties. This does not mean that adults with learning difficulties have to manage without help and support, but that they retain control of what happens.

Learning about self advocacy

Many areas have set up courses or training opportunities. Some of these aim to give people the skills and tools to take back some control over their lives, for example through assertiveness training. Others have offered a much broader approach to self-development, such as the Open University course *Working Together* (course number P555M; see page 115 for further details).

There are a number of courses providing training in the skills needed by self advocacy groups. Some of these are run by the self advocacy organisations themselves. In other instances self advocacy groups have managed to obtain access to training resources to help them with particular issues.

There is enormous scope for adult and further education to provide the kinds of training or learning opportunities that adults with learning difficulties want as they develop as individuals and groups through involvement in self advocacy. Self awareness, how to run a meeting and talking to top people are examples of courses that people have requested.

These needs have been identified by people with learning difficulties themselves, rather than prescribed by professionals. The curriculum should be defined by the learners wherever possible. It is not a question of professionals telling people with learning difficulties what to do or what self advocacy is! Neither should there be any qualification hurdles to leap. People do not necessarily need 'pre-advocacy' training before they can speak for themselves. What they do need is the chance to hear about the idea of self advocacy, and, if they wish, the opportunity and support to have a go themselves. Snapshots of self advocacy in action from around the country are offered in the following sections.

5

Self advocacy in South Glamorgan

A full-time self advocacy co-ordinator funded by the social services department is based within South Glamorgan's community education service. Twelve groups with a total membership of approximately 130 adults with learning difficulties meet in community education centres. Transport is provided for the majority. A further seven groups involving 58 people meet at social services day centres. Recent developments include:

- the formation of a group of users to develop user-led monitoring and evaluation of services
- video groups to explore self-image and personal identity
- developing user involvement in staff selection
- a self advocacy forum of 16 people, eight of whom have learning difficulties, meets together monthly to work on issues of common concern at County Hall
- one group successfully campaigned for indoor wheelchair access to new café facilities at the Howardian Community Education Centre. The group devised a petition and collected 400 signatures to support their case
- a two-day consultation about changes to day services was held with 30 service users
- links with People First, South Wales have been made
- a newsletter is in preparation to share news and information about self advocacy groups, who will be actively involved in news-gathering and editing
- a 10-week training course for self advocacy facilitators is being developed by a multi-agency team. It started in autumn 1992, and has received initial approval from the Welsh Joint Education Council.

Self advocacy co-ordinator Sonia Liggett comments:

'Interest in self advocacy is beginning to grow, as is the understanding of its significance by parents and professionals. Service users are increasingly discovering that they can exert influence over their lives. However, there are still many situations

*in which people are prevented from exercising choice, and this can
lead to great frustration and apathy.'*

People First, Cell Barnes

In February 1992 local journalists came to Cell Barnes Hospital
near St Albans in Hertfordshire to take photographs of some
pot-holes that had been repaired. The People First group at the
hospital had campaigned to get the hospital roads repaired. The
local press came to record their victory.

The People First, Cell Barnes group has a successful track
record – from getting pot-holes repaired to offering staff training
and producing a pack entitled *Our Lifestyles*. Rob Holt, who supports the group, describes how it used to be a 'talking shop', where
the same agenda items were discussed repeatedly without real
change. The group developed when training sessions were offered
on a range of issues, including labelling and disability; how to run
a group; how to organise a meeting; how to write minutes and
letters.

Another important development came when the group was
recognised by senior managers at the hospital. Members of the
group asked for and were allocated an annual resource budget of
£500 and office space, a telephone and secretarial support.

The group keep their own accounts and have used the funding
to support their work, for example:

* payment of conference fees to attend the national People First
  conference
* petrol costs
* hire of videos
* to support an annual self advocacy conference for people from
  all over Hertfordshire.

The group meets weekly on Wednesday evenings. About 15
people attend regularly out of the hospital's 400 residents. Each
month a senior manager comes to listen to the group's concerns.
Influencing management decisions is a priority. Each week, posters are circulated to all of the hospital wards with details of the

7

meeting. Reaching residents who cannot read is a difficulty. A taped version of the publicity had only limited success, and the production of a short video is being considered.

The group has attracted the interest of politicians and has been successful in obtaining media coverage:

- Granada Television's *This Morning* magazine programme has featured the group
- the *Independent* interviewed one of the group about life on a hospital ward
- the local press has covered the group's activities, including a campaign on the right to live in the community, highlighted by the recent refusal of one neighbourhood to have adults with learning difficulties resettled in their area. Neighbours clubbed together and bought the house in question to stop the health authority purchasing it. The group invited the people concerned to visit, but the offer was never taken up.

Back-up for self advocacy comes from a group of interested professionals and service users who meet informally as the Advocacy Promotion Group once a fortnight. Among the issues addressed have been the role of advocates and how hospital policies relate to individual rights and self advocacy.

Rob Holt describes the isolating effect of being located in a hospital. 'It's inward looking. We're cut off from what goes on.' Some of the group's most experienced members have moved to live in the community and have consequently left the group. This has meant that the group is evolving and changing. Rob Holt says: 'We have to look at the talents, abilities and strengths of this group and to develop our own successes and ways forward.'

Getting groups up and running: a catalyst for change

In the north-east of England, the Skills for People voluntary organisation based in Newcastle upon Tyne has acted as a catalyst in starting self advocacy groups in the area. Skills for People is a training organisation which runs courses designed and planned by adults with learning difficulties and other disabilities. By holding conferences in particular areas, and by setting up planning groups to run these events, Skills for People have brought together adults with learning difficulties in local groups to set their own agendas. A number of these groups have continued to meet and have developed to become independent self advocacy groups, such as the one in Blyth.

Individual self advocacy in an education setting

At the Paddington Integration Project (PIP) adults with learning difficulties are given responsibility for building their own individual learning programmes from a wide variety of options, drawn from:

- adult education classes in different areas
- courses run at PIP
- work experience
- leisure activities
- one-to-one tutorials.

Students can talk through problems and plan for changes in their lives, such as moving home or finding employment. Bernard Collier, project co-ordinator, explains that: 'What we hope to do is to give students a methodology for making valued choices to do with their lives.'

Resolving conflict over choices

Sometimes parents do not readily accept their adult son or daughter's choice of options. This led to one parent confronting staff and saying: 'You're twisting their arms behind their backs, forcing them to go to courses that they don't want to go to.' Students talk to staff about what they would like to do, but at the same time may be under parental pressure to do certain things in order to avoid conflict at home. How can situations like this one be resolved?

Speaking up on sexuality

Sexuality for adults with learning difficulties has been a taboo area in the past. Self advocacy is enabling people to speak up about personal relationships, to define their sexuality and orientation and to feel good about it, as the following comment reveals:

> '*Self advocacy means that I can be what I am and have the right to say to people that I am what I am. If I was a Tory, I have the right to talk about the Tory party; if I was married, I have the right to be that. It's also the right to feel good about what we are. For me, it's the right to feel good about my sexuality, which may be different to most people, because I'm a gay man. The right to feel good about that is for me the most important part of self advocacy. From talking about what we are and from demanding to be what we are, it's the only way we can feel good about what we are. Self advocacy is more than speaking up for ourselves, it's actually being what we are too.*'

Adults with learning difficulties are starting to get involved in working on issues related to sexuality. Advocacy in Action are represented on a committee about counselling on sexuality for people with disabilities. People First in London are working on a leaflet to help adults with learning difficulties think about their sexuality and are planning to offer training to relevant organisations.

Sexual abuse

Adults with learning difficulties who have faced and who are facing sexual abuse sometimes find self advocacy groups a supportive environment in which to confide their experiences. For example, several disclosures of abuse have been made in one college-based women's group. Dealing with revelations of this nature can present dilemmas for the person concerned and for advisers and tutors. People First in London are planning to work with the Family Planning Association to raise awareness of the sexual abuse of people with learning difficulties, not only with service users but also such organisations as Rape Crisis.

Equal opportunities and self advocacy

Some areas are offering space, time and opportunities for particular groups of adults with learning difficulties to meet on their own terms, such as:

* women
* black, Asian and other ethnic minority groups
* those with profound and multiple learning difficulties
* older adults.

A women's group in adult education

'It's for women. I like talking about everything.'

'Nice and quiet. Get on with the women. Can talk about something private and it's easier to talk to women.'

As part of its programme of courses aimed at adults with learning difficulties who have returned to the community from Darenth Park and Grove Park long-stay hospitals, Southwark Adult Education Institute offers a women's group. Tutors Yola Jacobsen and Kate Hall write in *Changes and Learning* about the course:

'The Women's Group provides an opportunity for women to share and discuss issues which are important to them, not only as women, but as women with learning difficulties, in a safe, supportive and confidential environment. The members of the group have identified for themselves the issues that they want to discuss and they are actively involved in the structuring of the sessions each week. For most of the women in the group, this is a new experience, which they seem to have enjoyed and learned from' (Changes and Learning, Southwark Adult and Community Education, 1992).

Subjects the group have discussed include:

* where we live and choices we make
* talking about our families
* getting upset and how to look after ourselves

- women's work and men's work – what is the difference?
- how can we look after ourselves when we are depressed?
- taking something back to a shop
- friends
- holidays
- what can we do when staff mess things up?

Women First

> *'I found it very interesting and helpful.'*

> *'I want to go back to Luton and start up a women's group!'*

On 9 March 1992, about 250 women with and without learning difficulties from all over the country met for a conference in Nottingham to celebrate International Women's Day. It was the first ever event of its kind. Workshops were offered on a range of topics, from sexuality to making friends. A pack is in preparation containing a conference report and a video. Details from:

Advocacy in Action
32 Park Row
NOTTINGHAM NG1 6GR

Women's group/forum in Camden
Camden is one area which offers space for women with learning difficulties to meet and talk together, and to try out new activities. A women's group meets weekly, and a women's forum for women with learning difficulties and women who work with them meets every three months to talk about what is important to them.

Space for black people to meet and talk

> *'I am a black person – I do not get respect from the staff. Staff should be sacked for racist behaviour.'*

> *'I want staff not to call me names which make one feel bad.'*

> *'I am a black person – I am always the last to be seen and heard.'*

These comments from a group in Newham reflect the voices of

black adults with learning difficulties who have had time to meet and talk about issues which are relevant to them.

'I crossed my culture out altogether. I denied my roots. There was no identity for me. I kept wishing to be white.'

This is how one young black woman with learning difficulties found that her cultural identity was effectively denied at special school. Providing time and space for black and Asian people with learning difficulties to meet and talk is increasingly recognised as important. Although progress in this area has been slow, a few groups have been established. One person involved says: 'It's slow to grow, it's taking its time! But you've got to go for it and take a risk.'

Apart from establishing and supporting groups specifically for black adults with learning difficulties, there is also an issue for all self advocacy groups and courses in terms of welcoming and including black people, and avoiding discrimination.

Involving people with little or no speech

Involving adults with learning difficulties who have little or no speech in self advocacy presents major challenges. People are struggling with how best to make progress in this area. Two example of places working towards change are described below.

Linsell House in Dunstable offers long- and short-term accommodation for adults described as having profound learning difficulties and physical disabilities. Ruth Kirchner and Glen Wheatley, who work for Bedfordshire Social Services, were aware that adults with this level of learning difficulties are frequently not part of self advocacy events. A 'Talking Together' day was held at Linsell House, loosely following the format of the APMH (Bridges) sessions held around the country in 1991. Keyworkers worked alongside residents, who communicated in the way they found easiest, which included signing. Together people worked to establish:

- things we like
- things we don't like
- things we'd like to do.

Keyworkers shared their own thoughts on these topics, too.

The Linsell House residents were able to share and communicate their views. Recurrent themes included having more control over their lives and dealing with bossy people. Frequent breaks were necessary as some people tired easily. The shared participation has had an impact on staff perceptions. Ruth says: 'The staff are full of enthusiasm and are seeing people in a new light.' Most importantly, the people who live at Linsell House have been talked with and listened to about their lives, which has resulted in positive changes:

> *Raj has an electric wheelchair. People become impatient and push him to and fro for speed. Raj was able to communicate that he would rather control his own wheelchair, and go slowly at his own pace. This simple but important right is now being respected.*

> *Helen was able to express how much she likes music. As a result she is now going out to enjoy live music and concerts.*

Speech therapists working in Somerset have developed training for staff and parents to facilitate communication for adults with learning difficulties. Signs and symbols are used to help people in a variety of ways, which include:

- making choices about drinks and meals
- making complaints (see page 42)
- understanding what is happening in their environment, from pictorial menus at day centres to symbols on wage packets and on group home rotas
- translating the minutes of the Chard and Crewkerne People First group into symbols.

One hundred and fifty co-ordinators have been trained to work on communication with adults with learning difficulties in the county. This means that the work of the speech therapists is having far more impact than if they were working with individual case loads alone. The principle that communication should be relevant and meaningful is central to the project, which is generating new signs and symbols from staff and users alike in an attempt to be responsive. Jane Jones, Chief Speech Therapist, says: 'Total communication uses a combination of speech, gestures (signs), pictures (symbols), facial expressions and body language to maximise the communication potential of individuals and groups.' A book of line drawings and symbols is currently in preparation. For further details, contact:

Jane Jones
Chief Speech Therapist
Sixacres Day Centre
Roman Road
TAUNTON
Somerset

The Bristol Advocacy Project

The Bristol Advocacy project surveyed the experiences of adults with learning difficulties involved in three different self advocacy groups: two independent People First groups and one centre-based group.

The centre-based groups

In Avon, it is Social Service Department policy that all day centres should have a centre committee, made up entirely of users elected by fellow centre members. These committees are usually supported by a member of staff; despite much hard work it has largely proved impossible to find an independent outsider to play this role.

Along with the members of the centre-based group taking part in the project, many members of Avon People First (the local independent group) were also involved in their centre committee, giving a large pool of people who have had first-hand experience of a service-based group. According to them, the centre committees all placed a lot of emphasis on discussing and organising social events:

'It's all about trips and fetes ... and barbecues'.

Fund-raising, whether for Children in Need, for Romania or for the centre itself, was also a regular topic for discussion. Helping others through raising money seems to be an important means for adults with learning difficulties to show that they are not just passive recipients of help, but themselves have a contribution to make to society.

Some of the centre committee have dealt with complaints:

> *'We told her there weren't no toilet rolls.'*

The behaviour of some users, the condition of transport, smoking and unsafe entrances were all topics tackled by committees. A few of the users complained that the centre committees were ineffective and insufficiently critical of the service (in the words of one man 'it's kiss the bosses'). However, the centre committees were generally popular; people wanted to be a part of them. The chance to discuss issues relating to their day centres was clearly valued by many people. As one person put it: 'We want the centre alive!'

The independent groups

Avon People First and Chard and Crewkerne People First members talked about their experiences. Some saw People First groups in a support and advisory role:

> *'We're the backbone of self advocacy ... if other groups have trouble, they come and seek advice from us.'*

Other important features of self advocacy for adults with learning difficulties in the two groups included:

- speaking up on your own terms: 'to speak up for ourselves – when we like, where we like'
- confidence: 'it gives you confidence and then people have confidence in you'
- co-operation: 'self advocacy is working together'
- working towards change: 'talking about things that could be done in centres ... how we could all make things better'
- a sense of purpose: for adults with learning difficulties actively involved in People First, self advocacy offers a clear sense of purpose and meaning.

Practical pointers: a summary

It is evident from the multiple and diverse examples of self advocacy described in this opening chapter that self advocacy exists in many forms. There are clear implications for tutors and advisers:

- there is no 'right' or prescribed form of self advocacy. There is value in diversity, and in having a wide range of opportunities open to people
- self advocacy means many different things to adults with learning difficulties who are directly involved
- self advocacy can be individual (a person speaking up on his or her own behalf) or collective (groups meeting and organising on their own terms)
- adults with learning difficulties need to define and direct self advocacy, and to have ownership of it. Advisers and tutors must of necessity take a backseat support role to enable this self definition by adults with learning difficulties to take place
- courses can help adults to hear about ideas and become more effective in achieving their aims. Adults with learning difficulties should set the agenda, not professionals. Adults with learning difficulties can tutor courses in self advocacy
- practical points, such as transport and a place to meet, need careful planning and resourcing
- equal opportunities issues are important to consider in giving time and space to certain groups of adults with learning difficulties to speak up and be listened to, in particular:
  - women
  - black, Asian and other ethnic minority groups
  - those with profound and multiple learning difficulties
  - older adults
- even within one area, different sorts of self advocacy groups can thrive and flourish. This co-existence and diversity is a strength.

Think for yourself

How would you define self advocacy?

Talk to other people and see how they interpret the term self advocacy. Include if you can:

- adults with learning difficulties
- parents and carers
- colleagues
- senior managers.

What self advocacy groups or courses run in your area? You may need to do some research to build a complete picture.

Is there scope to support the development of a network or a newsletter? How can such initiatives be user-led?

What are the barriers to self advocacy, and what strategies can be used to overcome them?

How do the themes of this chapter relate to topics discussed by self advocacy groups, courses and forums in your area?

Make a list of commonalities and differences between topics discussed by local groups. Are there any messages?

The topics discussed by independent People First groups were broader than those chosen by service-based groups in the Bristol Advocacy Project. Does this reflect experiences in your area?

Talk if possible to adults with learning difficulties in different types of self advocacy groups in your area. What do they see as major topics for discussion? What sort of things do they want to change, and what support do they need for this to happen?

References and further reading

Changes and Learning: A year in the life of an adult education project for students with learning difficulties who have returned to the community. Southwark Adult and Community Education, 1992. Report available, priced £2, from: Yola Jacobsen, Southwark Adult Education Institute, Queen's Road, Peckham, LONDON SE15 2EA.

Thinking the Unthinkable. Family Planning Association, 1992.

Our Lifestyles: An introductory exercise for anyone meeting people with learning difficulties. Pavilion Publishing, Brighton, 1991.

Training pack for staff produced by the People First, Cell Barnes group.

Chapter 2

Identity: The Self and Others

The way we see ourselves defines the way in which we view the world, while the perceptions of others are also important in building self image. For adults with learning difficulties involved in self advocacy, identity and labelling are key issues. Negative labels have often hindered or blocked opportunities for people described as having learning difficulties. What terminology do adults with learning difficulties themselves prefer?

Self image and labelling are themes central to the development of self advocacy. Labels can have positive or negative connotations. 'Mental handicap', 'learning difficulties' and 'disability' are terms which have been widely debated by self advocacy groups. How do people thus labelled prefer to describe and view themselves and their peers? This chapter draws on material from the Bristol Advocacy Project interviews.

Much of the opposition to self advocacy focuses on the labelling issue. Some carers and parents' groups remain sceptical about the idea of people 'speaking up' for themselves and are afraid that the shift in terminology represents an attempt to deny that people have 'real' problems, leading to a situation where the already limited resources going to this client group will be cut further.

The interviews and group discussions held with adults with learning difficulties in the course of the Bristol Advocacy Project represent a unique chance to explore these issues.

Which label, whose label?

There was almost universal opposition to the term 'mental handicap'. Not only was there general opposition to the term, but many of those interviewed made it clear that they would be particularly angry or upset if it was used to describe them.

There appear to be two reasons for this dislike. Firstly, people were very aware of the stigma attached to the term: 'We are not mental'. Secondly, they were also very conscious of what other people understand by the term; the unjustified assumptions that are made about people who have a 'mental handicap':

> *'It means people who are disabled and can't do things like other people can ... wash themselves, go to the toilet, eat, drink, walk, all sorts.'*

> *'It means the person can't cope on her own and do things ... and she can.'*

For most people the preferred term was 'people with learning difficulties'. This seemed, above all, to be because it offers a potentially positive self-definition:

'If you put "people with learning difficulties" then they know that people want to learn and be taught how to do things.'

This support for 'learning difficulties' was not unqualified. Some said they were happy with the general use of the term, but either did not see themselves as having a learning difficulty or did not like the term applied to them. A few people objected to all special labels. They wanted to be called by their name or advocated a neutral term like 'student'.

There are some important issues that arise from the comments, which are detailed below.

Language is important
Language can be used to control people. The existence of a label is often used as a justification for treating a person in a way that would not be acceptable to others without the label. For example, it is not unusual for people with 'challenging behaviour' to have 'privileges' (like visits to their family) withdrawn in an attempt to control their behaviour. In some instances people have been stopped from going to adult education classes as a punishment. Although there is no legal basis for these sanctions, and they constitute a basic abuse of human rights, in the context of 'treatment' they are often accepted without question.

Language can hurt
All labels mean much more than they actually say. Language is a complex system, where layers of meaning get attached to words. People then react to the label, and not the person; they make assumptions about the person on the basis of the label. All too often this has negative consequences for those labelled.

Self-definition can be empowering
Defining oneself offers people the possibility of seeing themselves in terms of positive potential. It also offers a chance to challenge some of the assumptions that others have made.

Labelling can have its advantages
The acquisition of a label can open gates to resources and forms of support that are not generally available. Equally it can offer dis-

pensation from pressures (both financial and social). However, these advantages tend to be two-edged swords. The community charge is a good example. Having to pay the community charge was a major concern for many adults with learning difficulties when it was first introduced. Exemption is available for the 'severely mentally impaired', but the acknowledgement of such a label has its costs. The fear is that this designation might be used as an indication of a generalised incapacity, and it is scarcely likely to enhance the self-esteem of the person involved.

However, having a label can also have more positive aspects. Self-advocacy groups themselves are a product of labelling. Getting together with people who have the same label can offer solidarity, and collective action can be a powerful way of changing self-perception and one's perceptions of others.

Since self-advocacy is very much about autonomy and self-determination, it is scarcely surprising that the issue of labelling has been of great symbolic importance to people involved in self-advocacy.

Learning disability?

That people with learning difficulties find 'mental handicap' offensive is now widely accepted. After initial signs that central government was reluctant to shift its policies on terminology, the Department of Health announced in 1991 that in future 'learning disability' would be used. In Avon the local NHS Trust had already agreed to use 'learning difficulties' in preference to 'mental handicap'. When the Department of Health introduced 'learning disability' they approached Avon People First for further guidance. The issue was discussed at length in one meeting and in the end only three members voted in favour of the new term. The argument that seemed to sway opinions in the meeting was expressed forcibly by one member who argued that: 'If you go for a job, and you've got the label "disabled" they won't give you a chance'.

In the eyes of many people with learning difficulties, 'learning disability' may be a big improvement on 'mental handicap', but it still has the disadvantage that it is a term that someone else has chosen.

A sense of self

Identity is not just about labels. The attitudes of adults with learning difficulties towards themselves and their peers were revealed in many ways.

Many of the people involved in the Bristol study related experiences that would have been threatening to the toughest of egos. 'They said to my Mum "I'm awfully sorry, but we can't have your daughter." I was so upset.' Abuse, rejection and patronising attitudes were all detailed, often with a sense of injustice. A few even described how their families found it difficult to accept them as they were (one woman described being sent to Lourdes for a 'cure'). The services, too, sometimes undermined people's sense of themselves; imposing limitations, judging and categorising (one man described being sent to a 'low grade' ward), or focusing on people's limitations. Yet despite all this most people still clearly had a positive sense of self.

This positive sense of identity was reflected in three recurring themes:

A focus on abilities. Rather than dwelling on their difficulties, people chose to emphasise what they could do. For example, many were keen to point out their relative independence: 'I go out and about by myself'.

Making a contribution. Many of the people in the self advocacy groups were making an active contribution to their communities. For example, Clive does work for a local wildlife group, while Delia helps in her local Christian bookshop. Voluntary work in nurseries or old people's homes was common. Many adults with learning difficulties wanted to do something that was valued by their community.

Helping other people. Self advocacy itself is often described as 'helping' other people with learning difficulties. Many of the things that self advocacy groups do (for example raising money for children in Romania) are focused around helping people less fortunate. Within their day centres, many people have a role that involves supporting or helping someone less able. This is not by accident. More than any other activity, helping others in some way confers a sense of being valued. It also emphasises the fact that most people with learning difficulties are not simply passive recipients of help.

Recognition of limitations

Despite wanting to be positive about their abilities, most were able to recognise and discuss their limitations:

'*I'm not very good with money.*'

'*I can't write and that.*'

However, many would only do so on their terms: if asked directly if there was anything they found difficult many initially said no. It was only in other contexts, where they felt more secure, that they would acknowledge problems. This has important implications for the way that people are helped to work out what kind of support they need. Above all, there has to be an environment where they do not feel under pressure.

For example, Paul occasionally has very bad epileptic seizures. Once in a while he goes into status, and needs urgent medical attention. In the past his epilepsy has been used as a reason for severely limiting Paul's life. Paul has become very sensitive about the subject. He is reluctant to discuss the topic, and hates people that do not know him being told about it. Paul wants to live more independently, and although he understands the dangers, his reaction to all the pressures was to try and ignore the subject, and a number of times insisted that he wanted to live on his own. Paul has only recently begun to talk realistically about what his epilepsy means to him. He now has a circle of friends whom he chose, and who are prepared to listen to him and take him seriously. They have started to find ways that Paul could have some control over the treatment of his epilepsy. Rather than dismissing Paul's ideas as impossible, the circle has provided a sympathetic atmosphere where Paul can work through the issues in his own way. He now recognises that it would be better if he could find some friends to share a house with.

Complexity

Many of the attitudes expressed by the people with learning difficulties are marked by complexity. For example:

Not everyone sees themselves as disabled. While most people accepted the term 'people with learning difficulties' as a suitable term for the group, many felt that it did not really apply to them as individuals. Even those that accepted the term did not necessarily agree about what it implied. Raymond, for example, was adamant that learning difficulties is 'an educational problem' and not a disability. Others were quite at ease with the idea that they have some form of disability.

Some are inconsistent. Like most groups of people in society, the adults with learning difficulties were not entirely consistent in their attitudes. For example, while most are very sensitive to the way that language is used to describe them, a few will sometimes refer to other people with learning difficulties in ways they would not themselves accept. For example, using derogatory terms (like 'dipstick'), referring to adults as 'boys and girls', or defining other, less able people as 'mentally handicapped'.

People may have ambiguous feelings about themselves and their peers. In the process of coming to terms with themselves, most people with learning difficulties will have had to face up to many difficult issues. They are certainly well aware of the stigma of their label. Not surprisingly, some feel ambiguous about themselves and similarly labelled people. For example, while some will emphasise their solidarity with other people with learning difficulties, others tend to distance themselves, particularly from people whom they perceive as less able.

Expressed attitudes vary with context. Again, like most people, adults with learning difficulties adapt what they say to their audience. Some are reluctant to express themselves freely in front of staff or families. Some will present quite a different front to strangers or people they do not know well.

Some are only just formulating their views. Until recently many of the issues around identity and labelling were taboo (except in self advocacy groups). Partly out of a desire not to hurt people's feelings, and partly because they themselves have complex emotions, many staff and carers have chosen to avoid the subject altogether. Avoidance and denial have been the implicitly sanctioned way of coping. Things are starting to change, but many people with learning difficulties have only just joined the debate. These complexities and inconsistencies reflect the nature of the world in which the adults with learning difficulties find themselves. There are all kinds of 'mixed messages' coming from their families, the services they use and wider society. In most instances they have managed to construct an identity which helps them cope in the often difficult situations they experience.

What underlies the labels?

One argument often used by professionals and carer groups in favour of retaining the label 'mental handicap' is that it represents a 'scientific' or 'medical' term, and that it should not be tampered with; it is seen as 'precise' and 'accurate', whereas 'learning difficulties' is 'vague'. It is true that 'mental handicap' is regularly used by scientists and doctors, but then the latter also talk about people having 'this thing going round at the moment'. If it is to live up to the claims made on its behalf, then the term ought to be based on clear, unambiguous criteria.

Approximately 60 per cent of people with a 'mental handicap' have no clear-cut diagnosis. Their disability is said to be of 'organic' origin (a medical term which usually means 'unknown'). 'Mental handicap' is often thought of as a specifically genetic condition, but it can also be acquired through environmental impacts. Perhaps the most common definition of 'mental handicap' is that of an IQ score of less than 70. However, many of the people labelled have not been tested, and the usefulness of IQ scores is increasingly being called into question. More pragmatically, a 'mental handicap' is often seen in terms of inability to learn basic skills like literacy, though some people with a 'mental handicap' can read and write. Conversly there are something like six million functionally illiterate people in the UK. Most are not seen as having a 'mental handicap'. Finally there have been attempts to define 'mental handicap' in terms of adaptive behaviour. Yet adaptive behaviour is not just a function of the individual, but also the environment. In other words, people who appear unable to care for themselves in one environment can often cope well in one that is more supportive.

People acquire the mental handicap label for all kinds of complex, often arbitrary reasons; it is essentially a socially-defined phenomenon. This is not to deny that the difficulties that most people with the label face are real; even, in some cases, severe. However, it does mean that we need to be much more critical about how we use such terms, whether 'mental handicap', 'learning difficulties' or 'learning disabilities'.

Public images: advertising and stereotypes

Advertising by charities for people with disabilities now constitutes a large, fast-growing business, according to a report prepared for the King's Fund Centre by Susan Scott-Parker. In the 12 months ending in June 1988 disability-related charities bought media space worth £4.25 million. However, as Scott-Parker points out, the ethics of this business goes largely unexplored, with many of the advertisements portraying stereotypes that are offensive to disabled people. Above all, disabled people themselves are largely excluded from decision-making on charity advertising.

Part of the problem is that an ever-larger number of charities are chasing a limited amount of money. To compete charities have adopted two strategies. They go to great lengths to establish 'brand awareness' amongst potential donors and look for 'powerful' images and messages. Although there is no evidence that negative campaigns are any better at raising money than those which portray people in a positive light, there is a widespread belief that it is necessary to 'tug at the heart-strings' in order to generate enough money to maintain the services that the charities currently provide.

The arguments surrounding a recent MENCAP campaign illustrate these issues starkly. The campaign in question involved a series of four posters intended to highlight the role that MENCAP plays in the lives of some people with learning difficulties. For example, one showed a blank artist's easel labelled 'life with a mental handicap' followed by a box of paints (labelled 'MEN-CAP'). Others followed a similar principle but involved paddleless canoes and empty musical staves. Many people with learning difficulties were enraged by the implication that they were 'nothing' without MENCAP:

> *'MENCAP must be up the creek without a paddle to be so desperate as to use advertisements like these' (People First Newsletter, Summer, 1992).*

There has been consistent pressure on MENCAP to change its name and logo. This has had some impact. The old logo (Little Stephen) has finally been superseded by positive images of adults with learning difficulties. However, MENCAP has retained its name, and despite being told quite clearly that people with learning difficulties do not like advertisements with the words 'mental handicap' in them, has persisted with the practice.

Steve Billington, MENCAP's Director of Marketing and Appeals, is quite clear why the charity has decided not to alter its title:

> *'MENCAP is a £50 million operation competing for recognition amongst 150 other charities. I know the name is not liked, but to throw it out with the "Little Stephen" logo would be to throw away 50 years of effort. Look what happened to the Marriage Guidance Council when they changed their name to Relate' (letter to London Boroughs People First).*

Many organisations consciously or unconsciously project images of people with learning difficulties. These all contribute to a greater or lesser extent to the wider public perception of this group. What kind of image is appropriate? The decision on how to portray adults with learning difficulties surely must involve people with learning difficulties themselves.

Practical pointers: a summary

Labelling and identity are important topics of discussion for many self advocacy groups.

Most adults with learning difficulties reject the terms 'mental handicap' and 'learning disability' in favour of 'learning difficulties'; indeed, many prefer to be known just by their name.

Image, language and labelling are complex areas, and there are inevitable tensions and differences of opinion between people, be they adults with learning difficulties, parents or professionals.

The three keys points for services which emerge are that people want:

- an accepting environment in which they can express themselves freely on their own terms, that values them as they are. A fundamental question all services have to ask themselves is to what extent their provision enhances or undermines the self-esteem of service users
- opportunities to make a valued contribution to their community and to do things that are valued by them and mean something to them. People do not want to be portrayed as passive recipients of 'care'
- a chance to talk about issues of identity. This does not involve being 'told' about their disability, but having a space to work through what their label means to them in a sympathetic and supportive atmosphere.

Think for yourself

What different labels and names do services in your area use?

Make a list, and think about the images that the labels convey.

Are they positive or negative?

Talk to a group of adults with learning difficulties about the labels used locally.

Which do they regard as positive, neutral or negative?

Do they agree with each other?

How can different agencies come to an understanding of terminology? (For example 'special needs' in a college setting usually has different connotations from the same term used in a day centre.)

Have self advocacy groups expressed the wish to change labels locally? If so, have their views had any impact?

What have members of the groups been called, and how do they feel about it?

The following is a list of some of the labels which services apply to people:

- users
- trainees
- clients
- members
- customers
- patients
- students
- consumers
- self advocates
- disabled
- people with ...
  - learning difficulties
  - learning disabilities
  - mental handicaps
  - intellectual disabilities
  - challenging behaviour
  - profound and multiple learning difficulties
  - Down's syndrome
  - special needs

People in self advocacy groups report being called:

- handicapped

- high grade
- mental
- low grade
- mental handicapped
- children
- backward
- mongol
- subnormal
- spastic
- retarded
- slow learners

Can you add to these lists?

Reference

Susan Scott-Parker *They Aren't in the Brief: Advertising people with disabilities.* King's Fund Centre, 1989.

Chapter 3

On Your Own: Self Advocacy and Individual Planning

What is the relationship between self advocacy and individual planning for adults with learning difficulties? Individual plans are becoming the 'norm' for adults with learning difficulties in different settings, from colleges to day centres. How much say do the people at the centre of the plans have, and what do they really think about the process?

At the start of this book we defined self advocacy in terms of a 'movement' and as a 'process'. There is a distinction between self advocacy as a collective act and people speaking up and taking action as individuals. Of course the two are not mutually exclusive; for example, through involvement in a group, people with learning difficulties may well develop the confidence to tackle issues in their own life. However, underlying the distinction are quite different visions of what self advocacy is about. Much of the rest of this book is about collective self advocacy; this chapter focuses on individual self advocacy. It attempts to:

- explore the ideas underlying individual self advocacy
- summarise the experiences of the people in the Bristol Advocacy Project in terms of the extent to which they were able to speak up and influence events as individuals
- discuss potential pitfalls
- identify examples of good practice or innovative ideas about ways of supporting individuals.

Individual self advocacy

When many people think of self advocacy, they think in terms of self advocacy groups and the activities of their members. Although this perspective does not exclude the idea of individual self advocacy, it focuses primarily on people who have consciously decided to 'speak out' or who associate themselves with groups which have taken up that standard. Hence it is possible to talk in terms of a broad movement that falls squarely in the self-help group tradition, and has strong parallels with other alliances (for example the British Coalition of Disabled People and Survivors Speak Out).

Yet for others the term has rather different connotations. Within adult and continuing education there is distinct tradition which has seen self advocacy primarily in terms of self-development, as a framework for empowering individuals. For example, Mariette Clare in her book on developing skills (1990) describes the 'core components' of self advocacy as:

- being able to express thoughts and feelings with assertiveness if necessary
- being able to make choices and decisions
- having clear knowledge about rights
- being able to make changes.

As she rightly points out self-expression is only possible when there is someone else to listen and hear. In this context self advocacy is also about a relationship between users and professionals, where the latter have a responsibility to (amongst other things) encourage and value self-expression by people with learning difficulties, offer choices and develop decision-making skills, and to act as an information resource.

Within health and social services departments individual self advocacy has often been closely linked to ideas about individualised service planning (often referred to as Individual Programme Planning, or IPPs for short), and the attempt to develop responsive and person-centred services. IPPs were developed partly in reaction to the impersonal, dehumanising nature of many traditional services for people with learning difficulties. They also represented a move away from a medical model of disability – in which people with learning difficulties were seen primarily in terms of a bundle of deficits – towards an attempt to see people as rounded individuals with strengths as well as needs. The various models of individual planning have been characterised by a number of key themes:

An emphasis on change. Individual planning was seen as the key to reforming services. By developing clear, attainable goals for each individual and the services they use the IPP would represent an agenda for change.

A basis for planning services. Information about unmet needs was to be fed back into the wider planning system, ensuring that the development of new services was built around the identified needs of individuals.

An emphasis on individual development. Many of the traditional services were seen as 'de-skilling' people and making them more dependent. A strong element behind the thinking of IPPs was the attempt to ensure that supporting personal development was made a central role for services. Thus the goals set in IPPs were not just to be about the services but should represent targets for the people with learning difficulties themselves. By moving away from seeing people just in terms of 'problems' and by recognising their positive abilities as well as their needs, the hope was that a much more positive and optimistic environment would be created.

The involvement of users and their families. Crucial to the development of more responsive services is the involvement of the users of services and their families. IPPs represented an opportunity and a forum for users and carers to comment on services and give their views about the future. Indeed for many staff, IPPs are seen as the main vehicle for user involvement; for them self advocacy has become synonymous with speaking up in IPPs.

Findings from the Bristol Advocacy Project

How far have the ideas described above been put into practice? The experience of the adults with learning difficulties reflected in the Bristol study suggests that there is still plenty of room for improvement.

The importance of sympathetic and approachable staff
Staff who were prepared to stop and listen sympathetically without being dismissive or judgemental were greatly valued. However, not all staff were seen in this light: 'I have problems with some of them'. While some staff were seen as simply not approachable, others seemed too busy to listen: 'I tried to speak to someone on Monday night. They just didn't want to know. They said, tell me in the morning. That makes me very cross sometimes.'

Staff who empathise with users are an important resource. It is impossible to legislate for empathy, but there are things that can be done that increase the chance that staff will understand and be sympathetic towards users:

- ensure that users choose their keyworker. Having someone whom you trust is important, yet many of the adults with learning difficulties in the Bristol study had not had any say in choosing their keyworker, and a few actively disliked the person allocated or felt that they were not sympathetic
- ensure that a central part of the staff role is to facilitate self-expression. This might be through encouraging the development of 'listening' or counselling skills, or by ensuring that structured activities are available which promote talking by users and listening by staff. These would include: making life story books, bereavement groups, women's groups, men's groups and reminiscence work.

The importance of users' views

Despite their involvement in service-based self advocacy groups many users did not feel that staff were asking them for their views on how the service should be run. Users would often get mixed messages about the extent that staff valued their perspectives. Thus while users were often encouraged to put their point of view, they were also aware that there were many issues being discussed by staff which were never put directly to them. For example, staff-only meetings were criticised by a number of users. Can staff meetings where no users are present be justified? If users are excluded because of confidentiality (for example, discussions on how to manage challenging behaviour from a user) then does the whole staff group need to be present? The existence of staff-only meetings serves to increase the gulf between users and staff.

Main criticisms

A lot of users liked their involvement in IPPs but many also had substantial criticisms. Certainly many users had very positive views of IPPs: 'I could say what I wanted'; 'It was great.' The positive features included:

- being the focus of attention and being listened to
- having some control over the process; for example, being able to decide who is invited to the meeting
- preparation beforehand for any IPP meetings; having an ex-

planation of what the IPPs are about and reassurance was important to some users
* seeing (from their point of view) a positive outcome.

However, positive comments were more than outweighed by negative ones: 'They just chat about you ... they should get up and do something'; 'I think I was pushed too quick – pushed into the frying-pan.'
These negative features included:

* the lack of resultant change
* not being listened to
* an emphasis on negatives
* a lack of control over the process
* pressure to make quick decisions and a lack of information about options
* limited scope
* the association of IPPs with past crises
* a feeling of being tested.

There was no evidence that material from IPPs was playing a significant role in informing the planning process, although a few day centre managers had managed to make some minor adjustments because of information from IPPs.
These findings highlight a number of potential pitfalls with IPPs.

A failure to focus on change. As many of the staff interviewed as part of the Bristol Advocacy Project acknowledged, the services are static and difficult to change. The budgets of many organisations are tied down in existing 'bricks and mortar' services and any developments tend to be at the margins. Pressure on resources makes high quality innovations difficult to justify unless they also offer cost savings. Undoubtedly, the inflexibility of many services is in part due to all kinds of structural constraints. But it is also due to a lack of vision. There seems to be an inevitable process in which 'needs' are largely defined defensively in terms of what is available; alternative options are not even considered or are dismissed as too unrealistic. To avoid complacency or stagnation the prime focus of IPPs must be about change.

Bureaucratisation. 'He said he wanted a job, so I rang up the day centre to see if they could help get him a place on a work experience scheme or something. They said "Oh no, we can't do that because he hasn't been IPP'ed yet!"' (occupational therapist recounting experience). All too easily the spirit of IPPs can become subverted into a mechanistic process that has more to do with the needs of the organisation than the needs of the users.

An exclusive focus on changing behaviour. In some instances staff involved in IPPs seem to see the object of the exercise primarily in terms of changing the individual, rather than adapting the services to the specific needs of that person. Similarly, the behavioural focus of much goal-planning tends to place the emphasis on learning basic skills or eliminating challenging behaviour, sometimes to the exclusion of other equally important issues, such as the development of relationships.

A failure to involve users and carers. The findings from the Bristol research suggest that IPPs are often implemented in a way that does not encourage users to express their point of view. If people who lack confidence or experience and knowledge about possible options are to be genuinely involved in planning the future, it has to be done with people they trust in an atmosphere that does not intimidate them.

'Tell them they don't have to have them.'
Over the years Brian has had some very negative experiences of case conferences and IPPs. At a seminar which included discussion of IPPs he approached the presenter afterwards to say: 'You forgot something. Tell them they don't have to have them'. Brian has started to think about the future on his own terms, and now has a circle of support (see page 51) to help him achieve his personal goals. Some adults with learning difficulties, like Brian, are wary of the IPP process. However, in Brian's area (and elsewhere) regular IPPs for all users are one of the few measures of quality specified by the local NHS purchasers. What will happen? Will people be forced against their will to have an IPP? Is it either feasible or appropriate for everyone to have an IPP at specified intervals?

Reluctance to make formal complaints
Most of the people interviewed as part of the Bristol Advocacy Project had at least some criticisms of the services they used. However, it was clear that few were prepared to express those criticisms direct to staff, and even fewer would consider making a formal complaint. This reluctance to complain had a variety of causes, including:

- a fear of the consequences of complaining ('getting into trouble')
- a feeling that to complain is not 'polite'
- a belief that they have no right to complain
- a fear of hurting the feelings of staff or getting them into trouble.

The 1990 NHS and Community Care Act specified that by April 1991 every social services department should have comprehensive complaints procedures in place. These procedures are seen by government as an important part of the strategy to empower services users. Yet no matter how good these procedures are on paper, they will have little impact unless service users (and carers) feel willing and able to use them. The past experiences of users and carers, and the attitudes these experiences have engendered, mean this will not happen spontaneously; they need active encouragement. Strategies for providing that encouragement could include:

Training staff. In theory staff are meant to know and understand the procedures and their role, which is to actively facilitate users to make complaints. This can be difficult (particularly where the complaint might be about other staff, or even the member of staff receiving the complaint!) and will involve a significant change of culture. For example, at a conference organised by a self advocacy group, one particular user showed none of the inhibitions described above but complained loudly and aggressively. The reaction of some staff present suggested that they were responding to the way he was complaining, rather than to the substance of his complaint. Some people are going to complain in an inappropriate way (perhaps by being threatening) or will reflect a general state of unhappiness by complaining continually about different things. It is important that these people are still taken seriously and treated with respect, and that help is provided to complain more appropriately or to uncover the real sources of dissatisfaction.

Providing independent support to people who complain. In the process of setting up its complaints procedure Somerset social services department canvassed the views of members of the Somerset Self Advocacy Network. Amongst the latter some felt they could complain to staff, but others felt that it would be difficult; they wanted independent outsiders who could help them should they wish to complain. The local citizen advocacy organisation just being set up in Yeovil was proposed as one possible source of such support. In Hereford and Worcester, this idea has taken concrete shape. The social services department has contracted with Hereford and Worcester Citizen Advocacy to recruit, train and support a number of independent short-term complaints advocates.

Providing information about complaints procedures to people with learning difficulties. Social services departments are meant to ensure that their complaints procedures are accessible and widely publicised. Yet in an informal survey Andrea Whittaker of the King's Fund Centre found only two examples of material produced specifically for people with learning difficulties. One of these was from Somerset and included not just text but the symbols that are widely used in the county.

Complaining is one of the topics illustrated in *The Residents' Rights Pack*. This video and accompanying workbook stands as a useful tool in its own right, but was also successfully used in the Bristol Advocacy Project as a trigger for group discussions (Allen and Scales, 1990).

Actively listening

Active listening involves more than just waiting for users to unburden themselves; it implies an attempt to set up situations in which adults with learning difficulties can talk about things that matter to them in a safe and supportive framework. Some of the options are described in the following sections. (See also page 46.)

Life story books or reminiscence work

Many adults with learning difficulties appear to have no 'history'. They have few possessions, and the staff who work with them may know little beyond the often perfunctory (if not defamatory) details in the person's file. Yet past experiences will often be important in shaping the way people react to current events. Making a life story book (Frost and Taylor, 1986) represents one way to help users recover and perhaps re-evaluate that history. By revisiting past homes, writing to seldom-seen relatives, collecting old photos and memorabilia and talking about and recording these experiences, not only do the adults with learning difficulties have a chance to be listened to, but the staff often gain new insight into that person. Turning the result into a book shows that the person's life has value, and can be a way for people to introduce themselves to new members of staff.

Bereavement groups
Teresa has lost both her parents. As a child she was particularly close to her father, and has still not got over his death. But she is a very private person and cannot easily talk about her feelings to the staff who work in her house. However, her day centre has started a bereavement group which Teresa finds has been a great help. For the first time she can really say how she feels without worrying whether it is an appropriate thing to bring up. Maureen Oswin, in her book *Am I Allowed to Cry?* stresses the importance of acknowledging and respecting grief. She argues that people with learning difficulties should be listened to and have opportunities to talk about their sadness in relation to bereavement.

Women's groups
See Chapter 1 for a description of a women's group in adult education.

Planning together

Shared Action Planning
Shared Action Planning, devised by Brechin and Swain, involves a plan created by an adult with learning difficulties working in partnership with a supporter. In Buckinghamshire, Shared Action Planning has been used by the social services department, with adults with learning difficulties taking an active role in explaining the scheme to other service users.

'Shared action planning begins with the users themselves, and proceeds at their pace', says Yvonne Wells, training officer in Buckinghamshire's social services department. Between 200 and 250 adults with learning difficulties are estimated to have their own shared action plan in the county, a development which began in 1989 in North Buckinghamshire. The advantages have been clear, as Yvonne Wells outlines: 'It allows people to say what they want. It concentrates on the process and not on form-filling.' Whereas previous individual plans had emphasised skills and tasks, people with learning difficulties in Buckinghamshire are increasingly using shared action planning to make choices, express wishes and to plan for their own lives.

A warning

The book *A Fit Person To Be Removed* describes the memories of 17 long-term residents of the The Park Colony. As Maggie Potts and Rebecca Fido recount 'listening to the reminiscences ... has made us uncomfortably aware of the injustices and the inhumanity of institutionalised systems of care'. They describe how they intended to read back each chapter of the book to the residents as it was prepared, but found themselves avoiding this task and 'rationalising this avoidance to ourselves by claiming that the contributors would be upset by the terminology used and by the content of some of the reminiscences. We discovered that we were in fact protecting ourselves against the effects of the care system we represent'. They add 'the contributors too felt at times acute distress when listening to each other's reminiscences'.

Encouraging people to talk about their thoughts and feelings can sometimes lead to revelations that either have disturbing implications (for example the revelation of sexual abuse in a service setting) or that unblock very strong emotions in the user. This is not an argument against doing this kind of work, but before anyone tries such an undertaking they should think about the issues and work out their strategies for dealing with such situations, should they arise. Above all it is important to be able to recognise when additional support or different skills are required. Are these resources available locally? What kind of support could be offered to help people cope positively?

The balance of power has shifted from professionals to adults with learning difficulties and to people central in their lives. Friends, neighbours or relatives may be chosen by individuals with learning difficulties to support them in their planning. The process can be slow and can cause frustrations to those professionals who are used to making quick decisions and to teaching lots of skills. Support groups for staff have been set up to help with the significant change in emphasis.

Adults with learning difficulties who use shared action planning have the opportunity to explain the process to other service users at special events. Staff are there only to support the administration of such events, which offer discussion groups on issues such as:

- who makes decisions in your life?
- past, present and future
- being in control of changes
- talking to top people
- being assertive.

Adults with learning difficulties play an active part, often taking on the role of professionals in simulations to convey messages they feel to be important. For example, one adult with learning difficulties feels strongly that professionals should not block aspirations deemed to be too unrealistic or too risky, but that they should talk about safer ways or steps towards adults with learning difficulties seeing their goals accomplished. Adults with learning difficulties have also played a central role in making and editing a video which will be used to train staff.

Caroline Field, a social worker, describes the benefits of shared action planning:

'Any framework can be badly used. But with shared action planning, the person decides where the meeting is; it could be at home, at the centre or somewhere neutral. We say, this is your meeting and it's up to you how you do it.'

47

Shared and self assessment

Sheena Rolph and Sue Cowan have developed a transition curriculum for adults with learning difficulties moving from long-stay hospitals to the community (Further Education Unit, 1992). They say:

> *'At a time of transition, it is vital that people are given a voice, given choices and are listened to. Our FEU work aims to provide a process, the Shared Assessment Process, which ensures that the learner is at the centre of all plans and programmes. The learner's wishes, strengths and goals are central to every programme and because they are recorded, whether on a simple form, on tape, in Makaton or Bliss symbols or in illustrations, cannot be overlooked or ignored, and are acted on by all concerned in the move.'*

Contracts and shared evaluations help move the process forward. Self assessment has been developed, stemming from the original work, and has opened up new opportunities for learners at one hospital's adult education centre:

> *'Self assessment. It surprises you what you can do. I didn't think I was much cop before, but I don't think that now.'*

> *'Self assessment helps you to move on. It had given me the courage to ask.'*

> *'Self assessment helps you to learn. You seem to learn more about yourself.'*

Care management

One of the criticisms of planning in the past was that people were assessed in terms of their suitability for a particular service, rather than in terms of what they needed. Some critics have argued that this is an inevitable consequence of service providers doing the assessing and that there should be a clear split between the roles of assessor and direct provider. This has been taken up by government in its advocacy of 'care management' in social services departments. Although care managers will still be part of the department they should not be front-line staff.

The practice guidance issued by the Social Services Inspectorate (SSI, 1991) identifies seven 'core tasks' for care managers:

- publishing information about the kind of needs for which services are provided
- determining the level of assessment required
- assessing the needs of individuals and relating them to agency policies and priorities
- care planning, by designing a package of services to meet the agreed needs for each individual
- implementing the care plan and negotiating and securing the necessary resources or services
- monitoring, by checking that service is being provided as agreed
- reviewing, through reassessing needs and checking that the service provided is still appropriate.

Care management shares many of the original aims of IPPs. For example, the practice guidance confirms that the aim is still to develop services based on individual need and stresses the importance of involving users and carers in the assessment process.

Care management is said to be 'needs-led' planning, but in this context what does the term 'needs' mean? Implicit in most models of individualised planning is a shift away from seeing needs as an objective reality 'out there' waiting to be revealed by the professionals with the right technical skills, towards a situation in which needs arise out of a negotiating process between users, carers and the professionals; assessment with people, rather than assessment of people.

Experience with IPPs suggests that up until now professionals have tended to retained the upper hand in any 'negotiations' of need. Although the practice guidance acknowledges that need is a 'relative' concept it still stacks the deck very much in the professionals' favour. For example, it defines need as:

'The requirements of individuals to enable them to achieve or

> *maintain or restore an acceptable level of social independence or quality of life, as defined by the care agency or authority.'*

Will care management make any difference? This probably depends on whether the lessons from IPPs have been learnt; in particular the extent to which the process is managed in a way that promotes participation.

A wider vision

Most of what we have discussed so far has been about service planning. Yet life in the community is not just about service provision; it is also about relationships, inclusion and involvement. Indeed, services should not see themselves as having a monopoly on planning. There are a number of ways of organising independent, community-based support to help individuals work out what they want from life and what kinds of help they would like.

Citizen advocacy

Sandra has a 'special friend' (Mary), someone with whom she goes out on a regular basis. Sandra particularly values her friendship with Mary because, as she put it, 'with Mary, you can talk about anything in your life'. Mary is a citizen advocate. She has no connections with the services and her loyalties are only to Sandra. She is not paid for the time she spends with Sandra (not even expenses). She does it out of commitment. Sometimes citizen advocates are the only people in the lives of their partners who are not paid to be with them. Mary was recruited by the local citizen advocacy organisation:

> *'Citizen advocacy works by demonstration. Members of devalued groups are put in touch, on a one-to-one basis, with ordinary people who have their own place in the community and who will listen to their point of view, respect their wishes, and stand by them to defend their rights' (Butler, Carr and Sullivan, 1988).*

There is widespread misunderstanding about the nature of citizen advocacy. For example, many staff argue that they act as advocates for service users, and that they know the individual far better than any outsider who has 'just walked in off the street'. While it is true that some staff do have very strong relationships with some users, and will try and protect their interests where possible, all will suffer from conflict of interest at some stage. Either they will come into contention with their employers (at which point most staff are forced to back off) or they are torn between the interests of that particular individual and the interests of other users. Staff also inevitably see users through a service filter.

Because of their independence and because their loyalties are solely to their partners, citizen advocates do not face that conflict of interest. Neither is it true that they 'just walk in off the street'. Recruiting and matching advocates and partners on the basis of shared interests is a demanding, time-consuming business. This means that the demand for advocates usually far outstrips supply. This has led to pressures on citizen advocacy organisations to compromise (for example to operate more along the lines of traditional volunteer bureaux). But citizen advocacy is about applying principles. The quality of the relationships is important, not the quantity.

Citizen advocacy is not:

- just for people who cannot speak for themselves
- about the advocate deciding things for their partner.

It is about:

- helping people decide what they want
- helping people say what they want
- helping them to be heard
- providing friendship and commitment
- providing links to other people in the community
- preventing abuse of vulnerable or isolated people.

Circles of support
In summer 1992 a small group of disabled and non-disabled people arrived in the UK from Connecticut, USA. They were members of Communitas, a small organisation dedicated to 'building supportive communities'. They had come to share some of their experi-

ences at events in London and Bristol. Communitas works by setting out to establish 'circles of support' around an individual with a disability. The circle is a group of people who agree to meet on a regular basis to help the individual accomplish certain goals or personal visions. The members of the circle usually consist of friends, family members, neighbours, church members and other people with disabilities, all of whom who have got to know that individual. Circles can and do include paid staff, but they are always in a minority. The emphasis is on inclusion, on recognising capacity (or 'giftedness') in everyone, and acknowledging that we are all interdependent.

At first the language and symbolism used by Communitas may seem rather emotive and distinctly 'American', especially to professionals who are used to a rather cooler, more detached approach. (For example, members of Communitas do not 'work' with people, they 'walk' with them.) However, Communitas is not about detachment. Those events had a profound effect on many who were involved in them, especially some of the people with learning difficulties and families who attended. There are now a number of circles for adults with learning difficulties in Britain.

Service brokerage
The concept of service brokerage started in Canada during the 1970s with a group of parents who felt that the interests of their children were not being met by the traditional services. Committed to the ideal that everyone should be able to live in the community given the right kind of support, they wanted a system that started with the interests of the disabled person. Above all, they wanted a service that would maintain or strengthen the links between a disabled individual and their friends and family.

Service brokers act independently of all the agencies which provide services for disabled people. They are accountable to the disabled people and their friends and family who have chosen to use their help, and not to the services. The role of the broker is to help the clients decide what support they need. They design and then (subject to the approval of their clients) negotiate a package of services from the most appropriate source, acting as a guide through the system. In many instances this may involve attempting to persuade agencies to be more flexible and innovative.

In Canada, the growth of brokerage was helped by the wider availability of individualised funding and direct payment. The Canadian government was either allocating a specific budget for individuals or literally providing money for people to purchase services directly. Direct payment in particular was seen as providing the ultimate in empowering users by giving them economic leverage; the ability to hire and fire supporters that they chose. In the UK direct payment appears to have been ruled out of court and examples of individualised funding are rare. Despite the lack of such opportunities, an experimental brokerage project for people with learning difficulties in Bristol is beginning to make some headway. People have come to the project from a wide range of situations – from a man with challenging behaviour stuck in hospital, to a young woman looking for something other than just the local day centre when her college course finishes. Although all have been dissatisfied with the existing options on offer, they have not always arrived with a clear idea of what they want. Much time and effort has been put into helping people explore the many different possibilities, and ensuring that they have support to help them arrive at clear, positive choices.

Practical pointers: a summary

Individual self advocacy is an essential part of life planning for adults with learning difficulties.

Individual programme plans (IPPs) are used in many areas. People interviewed for the Bristol Advocacy Project were critical of many features of IPPs.

Newer alternatives, such as shared action planning, self assessment, circles of support and service brokerage, are gradually being developed and used.

Adults who wish to complain about services may need practical help and support to make a complaint. Some areas are setting up complaints advocacy schemes for adults with learning difficulties.

Citizen advocacy partners people with and without learning difficulties and enables individuals with learning difficulties to have an ally in making their views known and understood.

Think for yourself

What individual planning systems are in use in your area?

How are adults with learning difficulties involved? Are they planned for or planned with?

Who has ownership of plans?

More participative approaches place great demands on both time and skills for all involved. Shared Action Planning in a traditional day centre has been compared by Steve Dowson to 'trying to hold an oriental tea ceremony in Macdonald's'. What are the implications of really involving users in individual planning?

Is the planning for services, or for people's lives?

What impact have complaints procedures had? Are people supported to make complaints?

Talk with a number of adults with learning difficulties in your area. What have their experiences of individual planning been, if any? Has the process been positive, negative or neutral? Have changes occurred in their lives as a result?

References

Peter Allen and Kate Scales *Residents' Rights: Helping people with learning difficulties understand their housing rights*. Pavilion Publishing, 1990.

Ann Brechin and John Swain *Changing Relationships: Shared action planning*. Harper & Row, 1987.

David Brandon and Noel Towell *An Introduction to Service Brokerage*. Good Impressions Publishing, 1990.

K. Butler, S. Carr and F. Sullivan *Citizen Advocacy: A powerful partnership*. National Citizen Advocacy, 1988.

Mariette Clare *Developing Self Advocacy Skills*. Further Education Unit/REPLAN, 1990.

G. Ducharne and P. Beeman 'One candle power.' In B. Mount, P. Beeman and G. Ducharne *What Are We Learning About Bridgebuilding?* (A description of the work of Communitas, available from Communitas Inc., PO Box 374, Manchester, Connecticut, USA, 06045.)

D. Frost and K. Taylor 'This is my life.' *Community Care*, 7 August 1986.

Further Education Unit *A New Life. Transition learning programmes for people with severe learning difficulties moving from long-stay hospitals into the community*. FEU, 1992.

Maureen Oswin *Am I Allowed To Cry?* Souvenir Press, 1991.

Maggie Potts and Rebecca Fido *A Fit Person To Be Removed*. Northcote House, 1991.

Social Services Inspectorate *Care Management: Practice guidance*. HMSO, 1991.

Chapter 4

Participation

Involving people with learning difficulties in the planning of various services which they use has become an increasingly important focus for many organisations. However, few models exist to inform ways of working. In this chapter, examples show that adults with learning difficulties can have a real say in both the personal and the political spheres, given the opportunity.

Power

We do not have the power. Staff, parents and some people we live with do.

Not having power makes us feel:

— Really sad
— In a grumpy mood
— Sometimes it makes me want to cry
— I feel like a little kid
— I feel wild with anger
— We get the hump sometimes
— We feel awful
— Miserable
— Rotten
— Unhappy and uneasy
— I don't feel so good and sometimes I feel ill
— Sometimes I feel a bit shy
— The staff do have power over us
— The professionals are always telling us what to do
— When someone tells me what to do I want to move out
— I feel upset because members of staff always tell me what to do
— We want the choice to do what we want to do
— Everybody wants to be more powerful
— If we felt more powerful we would be in control of our own lives
— Power gives you freedom

(By adults with learning difficulties from Newham)

Why is having a voice important?

Gives power; used correctly, this is good, but bad if used as 'brainwashing'. Having a voice can give you protection and safety – people's rights. A voice can sort out confusing feelings. A voice gives us the right to:

— Speak up for ourselves and others
— To take responsibilities
— To share experiences
— To put views and opinions
— To tell others how we feel, to avoid misunderstandings
— Avoid Adolf!
— To be friendly
— To avoid being put upon

A voice can be:

— A group
— Sign language
— Must also listen, hear and understand
— Learn how to ask
— Who can help
— Know what others are getting – so you can get your bit!
— Putting your foot down with a firm hand

If we did not have a voice:

— Nothing would be done
— We would not be listened to
— We would not have informed choices
— We would not have a chance to practise using our voice
— We could not give information to others

(From a self advocacy conference at Dartington Hall)

> *'Self advocacy is about changing things for the better. Self advocacy is not only talking about what people want in their lives but taking action to do something about it' (Andrea Whittaker, Supporting Self Advocacy, 1991).*

As one adult with learning difficulties astutely observed: 'You don't have to have an IPP before you can get what you want.' There are ways of influencing the system through collective self advocacy.

Adults with learning difficulties are starting to have a voice in planning processes – from representation on consultative groups to participation in formal planning committees. Other important aspects of participation include the involvement of users in staff training and recruitment and in service evaluation. The development of political awareness has been crucial in getting messages across. What ways can be found to involve people and what is the experience of such participation like for adults with learning difficulties themselves? How can services and staff adapt their practices to empower adults with learning difficulties, a process which involves a significant shift of power, emphasis and attitudes?

Messages about lack of power and the importance of having a voice are clearly conveyed by the words of the adults with learning difficulties from Newham and Devon which follow. Having a say about what happens in their lives is of fundamental importance, both for individuals with learning difficulties and for groups who use services in different agencies. Many professionals and advisers are currently wrestling with the issue of how best to involve adults with learning difficulties in a 'real' way.

This chapter offers examples of how people are taking positive action in different ways and varied locations – from lobbying to consultative groups and representation on committees.

Self advocacy groups and their influence

> *'It's worrying that self advocacy doesn't touch the real stuff in homes and day centres ... in some ways it's like the confection on the top' (Nick Rowe, Skills for People).*

Involvement in centre committees and other service-based self advocacy groups represents one way for adults with learning difficulties to try and influence the services that they use. Indeed, many staff see this as the primary function of self advocacy groups. The service-based self advocacy groups involved in the Bristol study certainly had some influence on what happened in their day centres. For example, in several the manager could not spend any of the money in the amenity fund without the approval of the centre committee. Other issues that committees had tackled included unsafe entrances, better leisure facilities (such as a new pool table), the purchase of a drinks machine, a request for more sport to be included in the programme of activities and complaints about cold food. Many of them were concerned about very practical deficiencies in the service:

> *'They pick up on things the staff tend not to notice, like the lack of paper in the loo, or plugs in the sink' (centre manager).*

Occasionally a self advocacy group has been able to achieve something staff could not. One centre was broken into on four different occasions. The users hated this intrusion, which they took very personally. The manager had tried unsuccessfully to get the department to install a burglar alarm. Finally, fed up with the lack of action, the committee wrote to local councillors, who were moved enough to come and talk to the users. Within a couple of days someone was down from County Hall to see what system was needed.

Nevertheless, while self advocacy was often felt to have had a real impact on the group members themselves, many staff felt that the groups had yet to have much of an impact on the service system. A few expressed frustration at what they saw as a lack of focus in much of the activity: 'There are a 1001 issues you would like them to be talking about, and there they are discussing a day trip.'

A common concern for managers was how to encourage users in general to be more demanding and less passive. There appear to be a number of reasons why service-based self advocacy groups have not really started to challenge the nature of services:

- many of the real issues and decisions were not put to the centre committees. Many users were conscious that staff knew things that they did not:

'We don't really have a chance to say how the centre is run. They [staff] have their own private meetings. I wish we could go because it is important to know what staff feel'

- it is difficult to reform something from the inside. Once people join something like a centre committee they inevitably get involved with the day-to-day detail. It is hard to stand back and ask fundamental questions about why the service works as it does
- people with learning difficulties may not always see being questioning as part of their role. As the earlier chapters show, self advocacy means different things to different people. For many, an important part of self-advocacy is helping others; hence the emphasis on raising funds and organising social events
- service-based groups have often been allocated a fairly marginal role; self advocacy is rarely seen in terms of users controlling the service ('It's still the boss who chooses'). As one adviser commented: 'There has been no real impact because users have no real power.'

The influence of People First

The relationship between independent self advocacy groups in the Bristol study and the service that their members use was, by definition, looser than that of service-based groups. Their role is closer to that of a pressure group. Social service departments and health authorities have often not been responsive to pressure groups in the past; the members of such groups were often dismissed as people 'with an axe to grind' (as though this was necessarily a bad thing). Inevitably the influence of the larger People First groups is hard to measure.

Nevertheless, many of the members of Avon People First felt that people were starting to take them seriously as a group: 'They listen to us because we have been able to do things people hadn't expected.' There was some evidence that they were right. The group was increasingly being asked by professionals (from both the statutory services and voluntary organisations) to be involved in all kinds of initiatives. Members have been:

- asked to help write a policy on sexuality
- involved in explaining and discussing the changes in the NHS
- invited to join a number of steering groups, management committees and planning groups
- asked to speak or provide workshops at conferences
- asked to provide input into training courses for, amongst others, GPs, nurses, social workers and day care staff.

This is all in addition to recent formal consultation exercises undertaken by the Avon Social Services Department. Members have undertaken all these activities with enthusiasm, and have usually derived a great deal of satisfaction from their participation. Members of Avon People First are now in a position to exert considerable influence, not so much through formal representational mechanisms, but through direct contact and involvement with professionals at a variety of levels.

However, success can bring its own problems. The demands on Avon People First are now such that they are largely responding to others, rather than setting their own agenda. Many of the organisations wanting involvement of members are keen to recruit only the more able people whom they have already heard speaking on the conference circuit (rather than adapt the way they work to suit some less able or articulate people), increasing the pressure on particular individuals and leaving them isolated from the rest of the group. The increase in pressure intensely annoyed one supporter of the group: 'I've been really bugged by the demands on People First. It's a bandwagon of user involvement that people are jumping on without putting anything in.'

The large, active group is seen as an ideal target by professionals who now have to start consulting users. Smaller groups that do not have a county-wide membership tend to be much less in demand. This was certainly the case with Chard and Crewkerne People First. With less pressure they are in a position to decide in advance the issues that they want to discuss. The small size of the group allows much more space for the members to talk about things on their own terms. On the other hand they probably wield less influence.

Participation in action

Planning meetings and committees

'Don't have meetings about us without us' is the call from adults with learning difficulties in Nottingham's Advocacy in Action. Co-workers from Advocacy in Action are represented on a wide range of influential committees, including Greater Nottingham Training and Enterprise Council and the Joint Planning Group. The views of adults with learning difficulties are also represented in policy formation. Advocacy in Action is advising CCETSW on the Diploma in Social Care and advising on complaints procedures.

People from Advocacy in Action say of their experiences of committee work:

'Initially we had to fight our way onto committees. Now we get invited.'

'We have to say, don't use jargon.'

'The first time for me, it was hard. We're trying to work out what's best, what committees we need to be on.'

'Just being there in itself has made a point. If committees are going nowhere or adults with learning difficulties are being ignored, withdrawing is giving another message.'

Prioritising which committees are important to be on, and which are responsive to and supportive of adults with learning difficulties (for example by sending taped minutes), is essential. A representative of London People First has been voted in as a full member of Merton and Sutton Community Health Council. Northumberland Social Services Department has a lead team which plans services for adults with learning difficulties. The team has been radically changed to include representation from four parents/carers and from four service users with learning difficulties, working alongside the reduced number of eight professionals.

Consultative meetings with adults with learning difficulties will enable the team to decide how representatives will be chosen, while the setting up of local network groups of adults with learning difficulties to feed in ideas and to exchange information is being actively considered.

There are, however, dilemmas in asking adults with learning difficulties to join formal planning meetings. In one county, there is pressure for adults with learning difficulties to be represented at numerous groups and committees, pressure which is being resisted because: 'We don't believe in asking people to volunteer for something that's not meaningful.' Instead, means are being found of involving adults with learning difficulties in other ways, by setting up a self advocacy forum and by developing possibilities for adults with learning difficulties to monitor their own services.

Developments in Great Yarmouth and Waveney

Within the Great Yarmouth and Waveney Health Authority/District, a core group of six professionals works with a reference group of eight adults with learning difficulties and eight parents/carers. Service users and parents are not related. Half of each group comes from Norfolk and half from Suffolk, as the area crosses the county boundary line. The reference group also has as members eight other representatives from social services, health, adult education, voluntary organisations and the Community Health Council. Sue Brown, district manager, observes that the comments from users will be valuable:

> 'Work is now to start on the strategy document on home support services and respite care. This should be very interesting, as we will be able to have the views of people on the receiving end of respite care. Traditionally it has been the parents' views which have been the most important in this aspect of the service.'

Clwyd People First

Clwyd People First is a committee.of 18 adults with learning difficulties from the six areas of the county, which meets monthly. Members are drawn from the 10 active self advocacy groups in Clwyd. A co-ordinator is employed for nine hours weekly to facilitate communication between self advocacy groups and to relate the groups to People First. This post is funded by the Welsh Office. Service users are represented on local planning and co-or-dinating groups, the county forum and the joint secretariat, which is the county's planning group.

Jackie White, the Clwyd People First co-ordinator, outlines some of the difficulties that have been faced in supporting the participation of adults with learning difficulties in planning meetings, self advocacy groups and People First:

Transport. There are few evening buses, so even people who can travel independently have to rely on volunteer drivers, which reinforces dependency.

Letters. Few of the group are used to having a formal to and fro of information.

Reporting back. Some groups do not always have space for reporting back and the work of People First gets lost.

Meetings. 'These are often timed for the professional and not for service users,' says Jackie. 'There seems to be a reluctance to hold meetings outside the professionals' normal working hours.' This applies to conferences too, which are often held mid-week rather than at weekends. Within formal meetings Jackie has identified particular problems:

> *'Official documents are often needlessly verbose. Few service users have difficulty with actual jargon, but often cannot understand the words which are used to link the jargon. Minutes often appear only a short time before a meeting (no matter how long and complicated the enclosures) and are almost invariably typed. In Clwyd a number of groups are now using tapes for people who cannot read, but these are usually prepared by the person's own support worker rather than the official issuer of the information. Discussion within meetings is sometimes exclusive, with no attempts to involve the service user or to make sure that she/he understands. In Clwyd People First we are trying to resolve many of these issues and are making some headway, slowly.'*

Cutting through the jargon

Judith Rose of Southwark Adult and Community Education observes that: 'Much more support is needed to facilitate the contribution of users to planning. Consultation documents are inaccessible in language, length and complexity.' In one case, adult educators in Southwark made their own questionnaire to enable students to make comments about provision.

Involving service users in meetings

Practical ideas for involving adults with learning difficulties in planning meetings are outlined in South Glamorgan's proposals for developments, which are underpinned by the major role played by community education:

> *Service user involvement in meetings: Procedures for meetings in which service users are to be invited to be involved should be reviewed. Care should be taken to ensure that: background information is available in a form that can be understood by the service user; all minutes and reports should be written as clearly and free from jargon as possible; the chairperson should take positive steps to promote a relaxed but structured meeting in which all members can confidently contribute. Workshops should be offered to existing members to enable them to address the issues of user involvement and change to working practice.*

Working Together

Many of the adults with learning difficulties taking part in the Bristol study complained about the lack of opportunities to work with staff on the issues that affect their services. Indeed in many areas there are no effective mechanisms for users, staff and carers to work together on an equal basis.

One possible strategy for meeting this need is to support the development of Quality Action Groups (QAGs for short). The role of a QAG is to try and look at and improve the quality of a local service from the point of view of the people who use it. The groups are made up of people who are closely involved in the local service – users, families and the staff working locally. Meeting on a regular basis, the typical group will work through the following cycle of tasks:

- deciding what an 'ideal' service might look like
- looking at how the service works now
- identifying areas for change
- taking one of these areas and developing a plan for change
- putting the plan into action
- monitoring the effect of the change.

An important element in the philosophy behind QAGs is that people with a stake in the service should be included in defining what constitutes 'quality'; the idea is that standards, priorities and directions for change should at least in part be determined by the people whose lives are most directly affected. The support of senior manages is important, but QAGs represent a 'bottom-up' approach to quality assurance.

While the idea sounds simple, in practice successful QAGs are not easy to establish. Genuinely working together often requires a significant shift in habits for all concerned. There is some scepticism about what a QAG could achieve. The Norah Fry Research Centre (Milner, Ash and Ritchie, 1991) has produced a pack designed to help support the development of QAGs. Based on the experience of QAGs from around the UK, the pack includes a handbook for all potential group members, along with more detailed advice and possible strategies for group leaders and co-ordinators.

Community care plans

One of the requirements of the 1990 NHS and Community Care Act is that social services departments annually publish their plans for community care, and that they should consult widely on these plans. In theory this represents a golden opportunity for service users to shape the way that services develop, although in practice this has so far not been the case. A number of factors appear to act against effective involvement of people with learning difficulties. For example, the plans and the subsequent consultation tend to be:

- authority-wide

- aimed at many different client groups
- abstract, with little concrete detail (the section on services for people with learning difficulties is often a page or less)
- not written for people who have difficulty reading.

However, it is still early days. Despite the volume of words written about consulting users most social services have little experience of systematically involving users, and if they can learn from their early mistakes, the process may well improve. Even bearing all the current limitations in mind, the committee of Avon People First was still glad of the opportunity to respond to a questionnaire from Avon Social Services Department. With a little support the group were able to include answers that reflected their feelings about the services they already get, and the ones they feel are missing, such as employment services.

Co-option onto joint planning committees

Many of the joint planning committees set up by health and social services have co-opted representatives of voluntary organisations. For example, MENCAP will have a seat on most Joint Consultative Committees that deal with planning services for people with learning difficulties. However, few include people with learning difficulties. There is as yet no compulsion for service users to be included, but the 1986 Disabled Persons Act does specify that when co-opting people onto the committee the services should consult local groups. It further specifies that this consultation should include not just organisations for, but also organisations of disabled people. None of the groups involved in the Bristol Advocacy Project has been asked for a view on this subject. This would appear to be the norm across the country. A report by the Social Services Inspectorate (Warburton, 1990) found that this aspect of the Act was widely ignored

Experiences of consultation

Not all experiences of formal consultation procedures are positive. For example one social services department decided to consult users on the issue of contract work in day centres. It was felt to be an anachronism, involving repetitive work for minimal reward. However some users valued this work. It gave them a sense of making a contribution, of doing something that was useful:

'There was satisfaction that you had a job for the week ... you would say, well, I've done that.'

They were not listened to; contract work has largely been abandoned. Worse, users were not clear why this happened. No explanation or justification of this decision has reached them. This is not to argue in support of contract work, rather to suggest that the chance for a constructive dialogue has been lost. The implicit message is that the views of users do not count; that others will decide what is good for them.

Waltham Forest: A users' consultative group
The Joint Service Development Group in Waltham Forest is supporting the development of a users' consultative group. The background paper explains that: 'Finding an appropriate way in which people can make their aims, ambitions and wishes felt has not been easy.' Independent advisers with and without learning difficulties are working to co-facilitate the group, which will be called 'Ask Us', and will have a representative mix of adults with learning difficulties from the community.

Recruiting and interviewing staff
A representative with learning difficulties from Advocacy in Action worked to shortlist and interview staff in a residential unit. He describes how he managed: 'It was hard. I can't write or read anything. We've drawn what I was going to say, and it went from there.' A user in Avon describes taking part in staff selection: 'It's good because you get to hear a lot about a person before he or she starts. I mean, you know exactly what they are like.'

Adults with learning difficulties played an active role in the recent selection of a new worker at Skills for People in Newcastle upon Tyne. They asked candidates to lead a discussion group on the topic of 'What is self advocacy and why is it important?' The adults with learning difficulties had decided in advance what they wanted to look for and why – for example the use of language which they found easy to understand.

One or two areas have offered training in equal opportunities selection and interviewing procedures to adults with learning difficulties as an essential pre-requisite for involvement in appointing staff. Lack of such training is now posing a barrier to the active involvement of adults with learning difficulties in staff recruitment, and has in some areas been used as a reason for excluding adults with learning difficulties from the process.

Training and assessing staff

Staff training and evaluation is an important aspect of getting messages about user involvement across to professionals. Student nurses join Advocacy in Action in Nottingham on seven-day placements. Adults with learning difficulties are responsible for the evaluation report at the end of each placement: 'We looked at their form and said: "No, we're not having that rubbish!" so we decided to do our own.' Advocacy in Action runs workshops for student nurses and social workers, and is working on an assessment to enable adults with learning difficulties to assess the skills of staff taking an NVQ in social care. People First in London have trained staff around the country. One of the trainers who has learning difficulties says: 'It's about getting staff out of being institutionalised themselves.' One exercise uses role play: 'We put the staff in the users' shoes. It was fascinating how they felt afterwards. They said: I didn't realise it was like that; I had no idea.' The staff became frustrated when, in the role of users, they had to be in by a certain time or couldn't watch a television programme of their choice.

Evaluating services

People First members evaluated group homes in Hillingdon and produced a full report. This important initiative is now being implemented all over the North West Thames region. One of the evaluators, Simon Gardner, describes how he recorded his observations:

> 'How I did it was that I recorded all my information. When I did the interviews I would memorise what people said to us, rush back in the car and do it all on dictaphone.'

Getting political
Arguably one of the reasons for the difficulty people with learning difficulties have in gaining influence is their almost complete exclusion from the political process. Many local councillors will have made decisions that drastically affect the services used by adults with learning difficulties without ever having met someone with a learning difficulty. Similarly, while professional organisations and carers' groups have parliamentary lobbying groups (MENCAP is acknowledged to be particularly effective), few MPs will have been faced by a similar group of people with learning difficulties. That is, until recently. Things are starting to change.

Members of the Avon Students' Council attended an Avon County Council debate on a proposal to revert to the use of 'mental handicap' rather than the term 'people with learning difficulties'. The proposal was defeated, and apparently the presence of the observers made a strong impression on the councillors.

At a meeting of Chard and Crewkerne People First, a number of members said they wanted to vote in the forthcoming election, but were not sure how to do it. They invited the local returning officer to come and explain the process. This was a great success; he was able to reassure them and encourage them. Most had few doubts about who they would vote for. They had been impressed by the response of their MP to their campaign to get a pedestrian crossing; his already sizeable majority was swelled by some ardent new supporters.

Self advocacy and the political process
A member of the People First London Boroughs Committee explains how speaking up for yourself to politicians can be effective in communicating problems:

> *'Say you had a problem and you had to go to a Member of
> Parliament or a councillor – like we did recently – you've got to
> learn how to express yourself and your problems to the member of
> council or the member of parliament.'*

Meetings
People First in Croydon have invited local councillors and MPs to their meetings: 'They've been to our meetings, just to listen to what

we have to say. And it does help. You know where you are. And then they know what you want as a person.'

Demonstrations

Adults with learning difficulties from Advocacy in Action in Nottingham demonstrated outside council offices in protest at proposed increases to charges for meals and drinks at social services day centres. Some adults with learning difficulties have been involved in political campaigning and lobbying. The members of the MENCAP London Division Users' Consultative Group have met Nicholas Scott, Minister for the Disabled, to discuss issues of concern; spoken at a fringe meeting at the Liberal Democrat 1991 national conference; and worked with People First towards developing a charter for adults with learning difficulties.

Raising awareness

Adults with learning difficulties in Walsall made a video called *For Ourselves*. The video put self advocacy on the agenda for local politicians when it was shown to a full council meeting.

Forming alliances

People First in Croydon are seeking to work with the local MENCAP society:

> *'We're meeting up with MENCAP to see if they'll change a bit of their policy, so MENCAP and People First will work together. MENCAP, I wish it would change its name. I don't think it's a nice name.'*

Practical pointers: a summary

Any effective strategy for involving service users (and carers) must have a number of different elements. These should include:

- aiding and encouraging all forms of self advocacy
- ensuring that there are many different kinds of opportunities for participation, geared to the varying wishes, skills and attitudes of users

- adapting existing structures to the needs of users and carers, rather than expecting them to make the adjustments
- ensuring that there is transport for users so that they can get to meetings
- providing support workers to help people before and during meetings
- insisting that all documents are designed to be accessible to users and carers (staff would gain here too). This is particularly the case with documents for complaints procedures. With longer, more complex reports, this might mean producing a summary, or a parallel version for users and carers. Wherever possible, tapes (or even videos) should be used
- service users should be involved in all aspects of managing a service (including training, evaluation/inspection and planning)
- providing access for users and carers to information, not just about services available locally, but about all kinds of alternative approaches. For example, users and carers might well value a chance to attend conferences that describe new ideas or services
- investing resources in participation, particularly in terms of providing 'no-strings' support to independent organisations who can help put the views of users and carers
- making time and space for direct contact between senior managers and other decision-makers, and users
- ensuring that there is support from staff to enable service users to take part in the political process
- ensuring that there is a framework for users, staff and carers to work together.

Think for yourself

What structures exist or could be developed to enable adults with learning difficulties to comment on, evaluate and plan services in your area?

What support is needed and who could provide it?

What are the resource implications?

What training is required for planning meetings and structures to be accessible to adults with learning difficulties and also to staff?

Are adults with learning difficulties in your area involved in:
- staff training
- interviewing staff
- service evaluation and monitoring
- planning processes
- wider change, such as lobbying and campaigning?

How can genuine rather than tokenistic participation be achieved?

What are the difficulties?

Talk to a group of adults with learning difficulties in your area. How do they feel they could contribute to activities such as service planning and staff training?

What support would they want? What scope is there to facilitate user participation?

References

Steve Dowson *Keeping It Safe*. Values Into Action, 1990.

L. Milner, A. Ash, and P. Ritchie *Quality in Action: A resource pack for improving services for people with learning difficulties*. Pavilion Publishing, 1991.

Walsall Self Advocacy Group *For Ourselves*. Video made by the group. Details from Learning for Living, St Margaret's Hospital, Great Barr, Birmingham B43 7ES.

W.R. Warburton *Developing Services for Disabled People: Result of an inspection to monitor the implementation of the Disabled Persons (Services, Consultation and Representation) Act 1986*. Department of Health, Social Services Inspectorate, 1990.

Andrea Whittaker, Simon Gardner and Joyce Kershaw *Service Evaluation by People with Learning Difficulties.* King's Fund Centre, 1991.

Chapter 5

Dilemmas Faced by Advisers and Tutors

People working to support the development of self advocacy as advisers or tutors face a challenging and demanding role, which can be fraught with tensions and conflicts. Confronting sceptics, supporting groups without dominating and making practical arrangements for transport are just a few of the headaches which are frequently reported. What are the main problems, and how can advisers and tutors network to share solutions?

Supporting the development of self advocacy as an adviser or tutor is a complex role. This chapter draws on issues and dilemmas raised by people actively working to support self advocacy. As Andrea Whittaker (1991) aptly observed: 'Being an adviser can feel as if you are walking a tightrope!'

> *'It's not easy – not for anyone who is involved, especially the self advocates. The pressures are immense' (adviser).*
>
> *'In developing self advocacy, there are so many areas of confusion, conflict and anxiety' (day centre worker).*

What should an adviser or tutor do?

There are few clear-cut models to follow in determining the complex and various roles played by people working to support self advocacy, whether in a tutorial or an advisory role. People have identified the following in considering some of the roles they fulfil:

- prompting discussion and keeping it going. This is particularly useful in the early stages of a group. Handing over responsibility for this role to adults with learning difficulties is important
- teaching skills, such as assertiveness or listening
- teaching specific tasks, such as how to chair a meeting
- helping groups devise their own rules for meetings
- supporting practical arrangements, which may include:
  - overseeing transport arrangements
  - booking a room
  - taking minutes
  - photocopying
  - assisting with letter writing
  - sorting out arrangements for coffee
- supporting the development of decision-making strategies. For example, one group decided unanimously to visit the local radio station. The advisers helped the group to think through who to contact and how to arrange the visit; when the visit should be made; where to meet; how to get there

- providing information about courses, conferences, books, videos and materials
- summarising, clarifying, recapping in order to draw out the implications of discussions and events
- supporting staff who want to learn more about self advocacy by providing appropriate role models and back-up information or materials
- supporting adults with learning difficulties in fund-raising to resource self advocacy activities, such as conference attendance.

Tutors and advisers working to support self advocacy are engaged in a complicated and demanding role. This is reflected in the following sections, which recount the specific concerns which people face, and are based on phone calls and letters received from around the country. The information shows that people are continually questioning their role in supporting self advocacy.

Conflict of interest: who funds the adviser?
Some self advocacy development posts are funded by organisations which themselves are major providers of services for adults with learning difficulties. This then generates conflict in that people with learning difficulties are being encouraged to speak up and possibly to complain about the services by someone who is an employee of those same services.

Rapid growth of self advocacy
Self advocacy is a growth area which is expanding rapidly in some places. The impact of sudden growth itself raises dilemmas: 'Things are expanding faster than people foresaw, which raises an enormous number of issues.'

A magic formula?
People with learning difficulties and advisers experienced in self advocacy have become regarded as experts by those who are at the beginning stage. Requests from professionals flood in, with problems and situations that need solving. The danger is that self advocacy is, as one person put it, 'seen as a formula. Do this – and

then people can participate. It's not so. It's a lot more complicated than getting a pack and setting up a group.'

A fashionable concept
Self advocacy is seen in some circles as 'the flavour of the month'. Supporters of self advocacy are sometimes viewed by cynics as people who are keeping up with the latest trends. The other danger comes where services which are promoting their image as 'progressive' use the term 'self advocacy' liberally while only paying lip-service to its real meaning.

Confusion about roles
How should advisers working in isolation resolve issues and dilemmas? If self advocacy groups employ paid advisers, who manages and organises whom? How does the relationship work? According to one adviser: 'It's difficult for anybody to know what you're supposed to be doing!'

Tokenism or real participation?
One adviser describes the pressure to achieve user representation on joint planning groups and management committees quickly. However, the groups concerned are not prepared to change their language or structures to allow full participation by adults with learning difficulties. This led one adviser to conclude that: 'Being there and participation are totally different.'

Pressure of time
In some areas, advisers are being employed to get user groups up and running, with the aim of supporting the emergence of independent groups and participation in service planning. However, the time-scales are sometimes unrealistic in expecting that groups of adults with learning difficulties will be fully self-sufficient in perhaps one or two years. According to one adviser: 'Managers grossly underestimate the time it takes, the problems people face and the complications of personal problems and institutionalisation faced by many adults with learning difficulties.' Another adviser reinforces this: 'I believe that the most crucial aspect of developing self advocacy is that it has to be user-led and to happen

at their pace. I don't believe a service can implement self advocacy, or set timetables for it to happen.'

The timetable trap

Steve Dowson, in *Keeping It Safe* (Values Into Action, 1990), describes the mistake of interpreting self advocacy as an activity which can be neatly timetabled a slot every week. His words of warning have clearly not been heard in some areas.

> 'Tuesday in our area is self advocacy day. Everyone does it! I went in to one group. I felt awkward because the staff hadn't asked the group if I could visit. Twenty people with learning difficulties were in the room and had been told to talk to each other. I wouldn't have known what to say!'

Examples such as this clearly indicate the need for staff development in order for staff to learn how to facilitate the development of self advocacy skills in a structured and sensitive way.

Encouraging assertiveness

In some situations – for example with staff or carers unsympathetic to self advocacy – it can be hard for adults with learning difficulties to express themselves. In situations where they feel safer, they are more likely to articulate problems and concerns. This raises difficult questions for staff supporting adults with learning difficulties:

- where is it OK to be assertive?
- who is it OK to be assertive with?
- how can the differences between assertion and aggression be conveyed?

This was described by one adviser as being like a 'balancing act'.

Continuity of group membership and support

When established members of a self advocacy group move on, this can present difficulties. One person writes: 'Various members left to go into employment and it was difficult to formulate a constant membership'. In the same locality, the staff who are trying to support self advocacy are themselves depleted: 'One of the main problems is shortage of staff due to holidays, courses and sickness.'

Progression for individuals with learning difficulties can inhibit or stop their involvement in self advocacy groups. As one adviser put it: 'The most articulate people leave to get part-time jobs ... or get pinched to advise other organisations!' This can cause disappointment for the individual if he or she can no longer get to a group, and can also affect the dynamics of the group left behind.

The need for confirmation

At one staff development workshop on self advocacy, it was clear that a number of the participants were seeking confirmation that they were going along the right lines in working towards developing self advocacy skills. One person said: 'I want to know if I'm doing it right!', while another commented: 'I wasn't sure I was going in the right direction.'

Conflict with parents, carers or staff

Supporters of self advocacy are often aware that in encouraging adults with learning difficulties to speak up and to make choices and decisions in groups, people may become more assertive in other settings, such as at home or at day centres. This can challenge the authority of staff and relatives and is a potential cause of conflict both for adults with learning difficulties and the advisers supporting them. One centre worker described the 'feelings of redundancy and danger' faced by parents in seeing their adult sons and daughters with learning difficulties becoming increasingly independent and confronting the taking of risks. A college tutor commented: 'Self advocacy is not always carried through to the home. We find ourselves compromising and going along with the parents' wishes.' Parents can feel threatened by their son or daughter's growing independence, as in the case where a parent said: 'Jane wanting to do more for herself makes life difficult for me.' The college tutor went on to say: 'We are constantly hampered in that students want to do things by themselves. There is not always support from parents ... You have to do it in little bits – just chip away.' Enabling adults with learning difficulties to recognise their rights is challenging for parents. One worker received an irate phone call from a parent who said accusingly: 'How dare you tell my son he has the right to get married!' These examples demonstrate the need to consider what support is needed for relatives and for staff in situations where self advocacy has generated conflict.

Getting the balance right

In one area, staff were sending large groups of users unaccompanied to self advocacy events. The social services development officer found that this was creating difficulties because there was then no space for dialogue or partnership between those who staff services and those who use them. Users are now being encouraged to actively make demands of staff and are being asked: 'Who can enable you to get involved in what you want to do?'

Support or manipulation?

'Facilitators can subtly manipulate decisions and directions.'

Several people described the tensions which can arise when staff working to develop self advocacy may unwittingly or deliberately control or manipulate situations or decisions. As one person said: 'As an adviser to a group, I am constantly questioning my motives.' Others describe how both supporters of self advocacy and adults with learning difficulties can be undermined by staff or relatives, who accuse advisers of 'putting words in their mouths'. Working as a team and monitoring each other's role is one way of counteracting this difficulty.

A 'dangerous' activity

Some staff and relatives still see self advocacy as a subversive or threatening idea. 'It can all go too far, you know,' said one service manager darkly. Those fears and misconceptions make the job of supporting self advocacy difficult. Some advisers have been unfairly accused of 'stirring up trouble' by supporting adults with learning difficulties in making their views known.

Self image and an ordinary life

One residential worker describes the value in promoting integration and choice through self advocacy. He explained: 'It's about parameters, control and self image. If people think it's right to be in segregated settings, they don't realise that they're being exploited or devalued.' He believes in setting self advocacy firmly in the context of normalisation, and being clear about the purpose of this link.

Progression

Some individuals, particularly those who have been exposed to a range of experiences, develop much faster than others in a group. While the rest of the membership are still working through some of the basic issues, some of the more articulate, experienced members may want to take things further. This conflict can be very frustrating for the latter, especially in situations where an influx of new members makes continuity difficult. How can the more experienced be helped to progress? One of the solutions may be to encourage links with the wider disability movement. This may well be a useful tactic in its own right, and will certainly provide opportunities for confident people to broaden their horizons still further.

Burn-out

An adult educator writes: 'While some people may feel that the group is an end in itself, for others they will want to move on, but I'm not sure that we have thought enough about how to support them in this. There is also an increasing risk that some people burn out through self advocacy – they get asked to speak at workshops, etc., lead busy life styles and become well known, then run out of steam (or, and I've known this happen, get pushed out). How do we support people in these situations?'

Practical arrangements

Getting to grips with practical arrangements is often something that advisers have to wrestle with. An adviser to a new group writes: 'We have only met on one occasion so far due to practical difficulties such as finding a room, people not remembering the starting date or transport being unavailable for people to get there. Although it may seem quite trivial I feel the actual practicalities necessary, particularly in setting up a group, need much consideration.' (See also Chapter 8.)

Facing negative attitudes and difficulties

Establishing groups in areas which are still in the early stages of developing self advocacy is particularly difficult. One person writes:

> *'The principle of self advocacy is still a very new concept in [a rural county], both to parents/carers, staff and especially people with learning difficulties themselves. It evokes strong reactions from all parties; some have been positive but to date the majority are negative – mostly parents/carers, who are apprehensive about enabling people with learning difficulties to take more control of their lives, but also some staff in day centres and residential homes.'*

People who have developed self advocacy skills are experiencing 'frequent frustrations' away from the group:

> *'They question the relevance of learning about self advocacy when their environment does not actively promote it ... we obviously still have a lot of ground-work to do both with parents/carers and staff.'*

Another person writes that the complexities of self advocacy can discourage people's involvement:

> *'There is some danger of people, which very much includes staff, becoming disheartened and shying away from developing this area due to the difficulties which are often created. I feel I have so much to learn about the best ways of tackling some of the issues.'*

The complexity of the issues

> *'The more you get into it, the deeper it gets.'*

There is a clear feeling from some advisers and tutors that at the start of their involvement with self advocacy the issues seem straightforward and clear cut. Closer involvement leads to uncertainty and confusion as the complexity of self advocacy emerges. The following comment from one tutor illustrates this difficulty:

'The more I do, the more I realise I'm working in the dark' (ABE tutor, Birmingham).

How do advisers and staff relate?

'The role of staff and advisers is complex – ideally all staff will be enablers of self advocacy, and it should determine the principles which underlie the service' writes one adviser. 'This includes very fundamental things, such as opportunities to make choices, through to the right to be involved in service planning.'

A sense of isolation

Some individuals are confronting the prospect of developing self advocacy in a climate barren of support. One person commented:

> 'There's nothing going on locally in the way of groups, nothing at all. Any resources are stuck far away and individual centres don't get copies. Tutors are open to the idea, but the information isn't there. I was going to do self advocacy through music, but the ATC didn't like the idea. I'm having to build ideas into my classes and do it undercover.'

Dilemmas in travel training

At the Paddington Integration Project (PIP), students and parents/carers are required to have a commitment towards travel training as a criterion for joining the course. Staff from PIP have developed a detailed programme for enabling adults with learning difficulties to learn to travel independently by public transport. This training can be threatening for some parents. Bernard Collier, project co-ordinator, explains that: 'Parents are often angry and feel confused, as they have never envisaged their son or daughter being able to do anything like this.'

Students can become disoriented by different responses to their growing independence. Parents who have agreed to travel training sometimes withdraw permission when it comes to the student making a journey alone. Bernard Collier says: 'This confuses students, who feel their loyalties are divided. Parents are basically not willing to accept the words of professionals when the safety of their son or daughter is involved.' Hence the threat from one parent to a staff member: 'I'm going to ring Esther Rantzen about you.'

One approach that PIP has successfully used is to ask students to take their parents on the journey they have learnt. This can reassure the parents that their adult son or daughter can cope with, for example, making a tube journey which involves crossing roads to reach the tube station.

Officers – or not?
The formal system of voting-in officers (chair, secretary, treasurer, president) has been adopted by a number of groups. As well as familiarising people with more formal meetings, the concept helps to create strong leadership from within the movement, through people gaining experience, confidence and status. However, in some cases this can cause friction and power struggles within groups, and can lead to a hierarchy which can be disempowering for other group members. The Talking Together group in Luton have decided on an alternative approach where the group members share out these roles. For example, those who wish to take it in turns to chair the meeting. On some occasions people share the task, supporting each other. This arrangement means that a number of people gain experience and skills.

Support for advisers

> *'There's a lot going on – but people aren't in touch with one another.'*

Staff supporting self advocacy are often working in considerable isolation. There is a need to make links and contacts to share information and ideas and to save duplication. Advisers and tutors need to collaborate and to support each other by:

- giving each other feedback
- offering support
- building networks
- sharing information, ideas and strategies.

Providing time and space for supporters of self advocacy to meet and exchange thoughts and views is something that tends to happen informally or not at all. Many conferences on the theme of self advocacy deliberately do not have separate meetings for supporters, on the grounds that self advocates should be involved in all activities. However, some advisers would clearly value the opportunity to exchange ideas and to share problems with other people in similar situations. As one person commented: 'If I don't get some of these issues sorted out, I'm not going to be much good.' Establishing support groups for tutors and advisers working with self advocacy groups offers one way forward. This idea is one expressed by a number of advisers. Full-time advocacy workers in London meet regularly for mutual support and have the backing of the self advocacy groups concerned, who understand that the meetings are not conspiratorial.

Practical pointers: a summary

Advisers and tutors have few clear-cut models and fulfil a variety of roles, from practical support to teaching skills for meetings.

People face a range of difficulties, from conflict of interest to pressure of time.

Conflict with professionals and parents sceptical about self advocacy is common.

Working as a team and getting feedback is one way of avoiding the situation where an adviser or tutor dominates or manipulates.

Discontinuity in group membership can present difficulties and can affect group dynamics.

Networks of advisers and supporters offer a way to overcome isolation and to share ideas and strategies.

Think for yourself

Have you shared these dilemmas and perhaps experienced others? Make a note of them if it would be helpful.

What strategies have you found helpful in dealing with difficulties?

Are there others that you could try?

Where do you get your personal support from?

Is it adequate? Are there other possible sources of support?

Are there regular opportunities to share successes and difficulties with other advisers or tutors?

What scope is there for networking locally and regionally with other supporters of self advocacy?

How can the role of advisers and tutors be monitored and evaluated?

What do self advocacy groups in your area think about the support they receive?

How can adults with learning difficulties be helped to say what they want from advisers?

Talk to a group of adults with learning difficulties and see what their perceptions are.

References

Steve Dowson *Keeping It Safe*. Values into Action, 1990.

Andrea Whittaker (editor) *Supporting Self Advocacy*. King's Fund Centre, 1991.

Chapter 6

Perceptions and Relationships: Family Life and Self Advocacy

The emergence of self advocacy by adults with learning difficulties inevitably impacts on family life. Here parents talk openly about what it has meant for their adult son or daughter to be involved with a self advocacy group. Views are also presented from the perspective of a groups of adults with learning difficulties.

> *'For 20 years my son has come home and gone upstairs to play his tapes. Yesterday he came back and said he wanted to go to the pub!' (irate parent quoted by day centre manager).*

How do parents view self advocacy? And how do adults with learning difficulties view their relationships with families in the context of their involvement in self advocacy? Discussion groups and interviews in Bedfordshire and Bristol provided the material for this section.

Parents and self advocacy

How do parents of adults with learning difficulties see self advocacy, and how do they perceive its impact on their sons' and daughters' lives? Two discussion groups were held in which 11 parents talked about their views in relation to their son or daughter's involvement in a self advocacy group.

Some parents were clear about the benefits of self advocacy, as the following comments reveal:

> *'It's benefited Matthew enormously. He is more confident in all sorts of situations ... It's about being treated as an adult. It's very difficult for us to treat him as an adult, as his parents.'*

> *'I think they benefit any time they're with others and can talk about what they want to. I mean, nobody ever bothers to ask them what they think, but they do up there [at the group], they can say it.'*

> *'Self advocacy is about viewing yourself in a positive way.'*

> *'Heather's got lots of strengths and a lot of confidence from the group.'*

Others understood and supported the concept, but were resistant to the label 'self advocacy'.

> *Mrs Brown: 'What is it, what's advocacy?'*
> *Mrs Fletcher: 'Thinking for yourself.'*
> *Mrs Brown: 'Why the hell don't they say so? I mean, why put those damn great words in?'*

One parent was unsure how her daughter saw the self advocacy group: 'I don't know if it's benefited Sarah. I think she sees it more as a social club.' Another said: 'They like going – they love going, they really do. They enjoy it. I'm not saying they understand what it's about all the time, because they don't. It's sometimes above their heads.'

An important aspect of people's lives

It was evident that the self advocacy group is important to the participants, and this is conveyed to parents in different ways. Most group members keep minutes carefully in a file and share these with their parents:

> *'Being involved in what he sees as adult activities – to have an actual file with his papers in ... to go to meetings when he knows that mum and dad are always going to meetings of one kind or another. It's very important.'*

> *'Having documents – the same as we have.'*

> *'They come and talk about it. I don't know that Jack talks very long. He says yes, we had a lovely time, yes I did talk, Paula [another self advocate] helped me. Then the date for the next meeting goes straight up on the refrigerator and he goes upstairs and talks to himself about it.'*

Spin-offs from involvement in self advocacy

Some parents reported an increased confidence in their sons and daughters from involvement with the group, which they felt had spilled over into other areas of their lives. Examples were given of increased assertiveness in everyday life:

> *Michael fell over an uneven paving slab. He went straight to the town hall and complained about the state of the pavements and his torn trousers. The first his parents knew of it was when a town hall official rang to ask if Michael had suffered any injuries and what expenses he wished to claim.*

93

Heather had a new camera and was having difficulty in putting in a new film. She went into a greengrocers and asked for help, which was willingly given.

Martin occasionally becomes upset. Since he joined the group, he is now more likely to say what is troubling him at home.

Jane has developed social skills through her involvement with the group. She has learnt to use buses to travel to meetings on her own, and to make social arrangements, such as meeting friends for coffee in town before going to self advocacy meetings and conferences.

Risk-taking

Some parents acknowledged that increased confidence brings risks too. Sarah had an 'unpleasant incident' with a man at the bus station four years ago. She has not been out unaccompanied since: 'Things were getting a bit dodgy. She is too trusting. We feel we can't really let her out on her own.'

Partents acknowledge that encouraging confidence is double-edged. 'There are dangers also in this. You can't assume that everybody is going to be generous or easy or even reliable in their approaches. There have been one or two incidents in which Michael has got himself into really quite a mess.'

One parent talked eloquently about her sorrow that her daughter was denied education, and about the subsequent shift in approach which seems to compromise parents:

'When they were little, we were told to love them, they couldn't be educated. We had to sign that they couldn't be educated – we had to sign the education papers. It broke my heart. They said: "Just love them, give them as much love as you can", and you do. You make sure they don't burn themselves and other things like that. And then, when they grow older, we're "too protective"!'

Choices at home

Parents reported a range of choices made by their sons and daughters at home, particularly in relation to leisure time, which included:

- jigsaws
- playing the organ at the local church
- embroidery and knitting
- shopping
- walking the dog
- watching *Thunderbirds* and *Dr Who*
- doing exercises each day
- choosing food and clothes
- scrapbooks
- going out for trips by bus
- choosing wallpaper.

Heather made the choice to go and see her brother in Australia. 'She saved up every penny for her fare' said her mother. It was Heather's determination to go that helped to encourage her mother to make the trip as well.

Choices at the day centre

Parents felt that by comparison, choices about day centre activities were extremely limited:

> 'They don't get asked anything at the centre. They're just sitting round doing nothing all the time. It's completely frustrating. It's frustrating for us and frustrating for them.'

> 'They have no choices at the centre. No choice at all.'

Participation and consultation

Parents generally felt that centres did not offer users a chance to give feedback or comment: 'I don't think they get the chance to tell staff what they think.' Others felt that the self advocacy group offered a supportive atmosphere for people to speak up, in contrast to the centres: 'You're all interested in what they really want. I don't think they have the same feeling at work.'

There was concern as to whether the views of adults with learning difficulties were being heard and acted upon by services:

> *'Do the authorities listen when they say what they'd like to be done?'*

> *'They've got a good self-image but at the same time they're not seeing their dreams accomplished and they haven't got a platform. County Hall must really hear from this group that there is a large group of people who need more realistic opportunities.'*

There was also a recognition that where parents themselves had been occasionally consulted about services, nothing had changed as a result:

> *'Authorities haven't got a clue: we get very cross. We fill in forms. We've being doing it for years and you've got nothing. It's a complete waste of time. They say "lovely" and then they go straight back and forget you.'*

Labelling

Parents had diverse and strong views about labelling. Some disliked the move towards adopting the term 'learning difficulties', whereas others positively welcomed it, as the following comments reveal:

> *'Learning difficulties. It's a silly thing to change it to. What are we trying to do – hide it under the pillow? They're mentally handicapped. What's wrong with it? It's a perfectly good name.'*

> *'I think probably mental handicap has got a detrimental effect on a good number of people. The more recent concept of difficulty in learning is very, very much better.'*

One parent disliked being labelled himself:

> *'I don't really like being called a carer. I find that word rather offensive and I don't know why. That's not to say that I don't care!'*

Other parents also objected to other 'service labels':

'The label I really hate and most parents hate is challenging behaviour. It gives the general public completely the wrong idea about the people it labels. It does them a great disservice. We can all show signs of challenging behaviour at times!'

'Clients! What a damn silly name to call them.'

One person also felt that labels were not always positive:

'Everybody concerned with services must look at the glibness of labels and the insulting terms of reference we apply to people.'

Lastly, a parent voiced the opinion that as time passes, so labels will be tried out and discarded in favour of new terminology:

'I think any new word that is imported to give a different feel to a situation will accumulate associations as time passes and will inevitably then become objectionable in its time and will have to be changed again.'

Room for expansion

A number of parents pointed out that the self advocacy group attended by their sons and daughters only catered for a small number of people. They felt that there was great scope for expanding opportunities for self advocacy:

'I think a lot of them would query things, given a chance. This is only a small group you have every month. If there were more groups they could state their case easier.'

'I was wondering if it was possible to have any sessions in the centres themselves, in daytime hours, with people coming from other centres.'

'They could do this at the centre – get them all together and let them talk.'

Scope for working together and a dialogue

One parent expressed the view that parents would be prepared to support the group and to work together to push for change, if the group so wished:

> *'It might be useful to have parents to use as lobbyists, to push from outside. The group might feel that we as parents could be useful to them.'*

An adviser who had joined the discussion group as an observer found that listening to the parents completely changed her views. Whereas before she had seen them as the 'enemy', the session drastically changed her viewpoint as she realised with a jolt that: 'We're all on the same side, really!'

The Bristol Advocacy Project: family life and self advocacy

Many of the adults with learning difficulties who took part in the Bristol study were living at home with their families. Most of them had positive things to say about their life at home, often describing how they had established a degree of privacy and independence within the household (for example through having their own room). Relatively few were thinking of leaving home. However, they also described a number of tensions. Issues relating to risk-taking, where parents played a major role in determining what their adult sons or daughters could or could not do, frequently generated conflict:

> *'Sometimes they [centre staff] try to get us like catching buses on our own, and I've been told not to. When I had my IPP my mum brought it up. She didn't want me to go on the buses.'*

> *'I enjoy cooking, but I find at home they don't let me do the cooking and use the oven.'*

Relationships are sometimes constrained by parental involvement.

> *'When I was younger, I met this boy and my mother said no, he's*

not your type, I can see he's not your cup of tea and it won't last long. That's her opinion. My opinion was to give him a chance. She made me give him up.'

Self advocacy enables adults with learning difficulties to become assertive and confident in group meetings and at day centres, but in some cases this increased sense of self is not carried over into the home environment. This can lead to a 'double life', where the sense of self-determination stops at the front door of the family home.

Consciously or unconsciously, services tend to keep families at arm's length. This approach has consequences at a range of different levels: as families may never get to see the adult with learning difficulties in settings outside the home, there is little scope for them to reassess their perceptions. There is a danger that their view will be dominated by perceptions of past incapacities rather than the potential for development.

However, families are often expected to make instant adaptations to shifts in policy. When one woman was moved to a long-stay hospital in the early 1970s, her family remember being told 'this is the last move she will have to make'. Fifteen years later they were suddenly told that their daughter was likely to move to a social service hostel. The professionals had a decade and a half to get used to ideas about community care, but families were almost completely absent from the debate.

Home life was not a subject regularly discussed in the self advocacy groups. There was little dialogue between the self advocates and carers' organisations (such as local MENCAP groups). A few self advocates saw their involvement in the groups as something that was very much theirs; something private which they did not necessarily want to share with their families. One man kept his notes in a file marked 'secret', and another woman had chosen not to tell her mother that she had been elected to her centre committee.

With such gulfs there is the potential for much misunderstanding and conflict to arise. Trying to foster a constructive dialogue between parents and self advocacy groups is one way of resolving some of these conflicts of interest.

Practical pointers: a summary

Of the 11 parents interviewed, the majority were positive towards and supportive of their son or daughter's involvement in self advocacy.

Parents reported increased self confidence and assertiveness.

Parents worried about risk-taking and about the limited choice of day service options available.

Labelling and terminology was as much an issue for parents as for adults with learning difficulties (see Chapter 2). Labels such as 'clients', 'challenging behaviour' and 'carer' were debated, as was the term 'learning difficulties'.

Parents felt that there was scope to expand opportunities for self advocacy.

Although many adults with learning difficulties interviewed for the Bristol Advocacy Project were happy at home, others had been constrained by parental attitudes.

Fostering a constructive attitude between parent groups and self advocacy groups offers a way forward.

Think for yourself

What support and what barriers have you found in attitudes towards self advocacy expressed by staff and by parents?

Is there scope for awareness-raising and training? If so, how can adults with learning difficulties play an active role?

Education for parents/relatives in relation to self advocacy is important. What opportunities exist locally, and is there room for informal support groups around the theme of 'letting go'?

Is there scope for parents' groups and self advocacy groups to work together for change on particular topics? How can constructive dialogues and working relationships be developed between managers, staff, parents and self advocacy groups?

Quality Action Groups offer a structured way for parents/carers, adults with learning difficulties and staff to discuss, review and plan together. Is this model of working one that is being used, or could be used, locally?

Is self advocacy used as an excuse by services to ignore the views of parents and relatives?

Talk with several parents in your area. What are their perspectives on self advocacy?

Further reading

Ann Richardson and Jane Ritchie *Letting Go*. Open University Press, 1989.

Alison Wertheimer *Self-Advocacy and Parents: The impact of self-advocacy on the parents of young people with disabilities*. Further Education Unit, Working Together Series, 1989.

Chapter 7

Working Towards Supporting Self Advocacy

Advice and handy hints from advisers and supporters offer the basis for reflection in this final chapter: from expecting hiccups to enabling adults with learning difficulties to tutor self advocacy courses. A checklist offers a summary of the main themes of this book to relate to self advocacy in your own area.

Practical points from advisers and tutors are drawn together in this section, together with checklists for reflection and action. The shared experience provides a starting point for consideration or confirmation of ideas.

Support for self advocacy

It takes time
Allowing plenty of time is essential. Nick Rowe of Skills for People says: 'Everybody wants to go too fast! Then they get frustrated. It takes time – it takes longer than you expect ... You have to fight off demands to go too quickly and say "This is going to take longer than you think".'

Expect hiccups
Nick Rowe says: 'You've got to put up with the chaos. It won't work smoothly.' This is echoed by Kit Roberts from Walsall: 'Life is full of ragged edges: nothing is smooth.'

Build a team of supporters
'It's tremendously helpful to work as a team ... we get really worn out', comments NIck Rowe.

Providing transport
At Skills for People, it is a priority to provide transport for adults with learning difficulties and other disabilities to get to and from planning meetings. Transport is the biggest expense after salaries, and costs an estimated £10,000 a year.

Making information accessible
At Skills for People, the minutes of meetings are tape-recorded. In Somerset, one self advocacy group uses symbols to support the written minutes.

Practical support
Skills for People provide signers as required for people who use signing systems. People with physical disabilities are assigned extra help if needed.

Size of group

The size of the group determines the scope and nature of the discussions that can take place, while the size of the venue may restrict membership. Avon People First recently had 60 people turning up for a meeting. Small groups of up to eight or nine people have enabled discussion in greater depth on selected topics. The Talking Together group in Luton has a stable membership of 12 people. The group feels that it currently wants to stay that size, to enable all members to have a say at the monthly meeting.

Planning for participation

Attention to the timing and location of meetings is vital. Sue Brown, District Manager for Disability Services in Norfolk, describes how careful planning has made participation by adults with learning difficulties and parents/carers a reality in the Great Yarmouth and Waveney Health Authority area (see also page 65):

> *'Care has been taken to encourage full participation by all ... We meet in a building which is wheelchair accessible from 11.00 am to 3.00 pm. This means parents find it easy to attend. It minimises travel problems for service users, although we do provide transport for anyone who needs it. We have a buffet lunch which encourages informal debate and allows time for everyone to "warm up" and participate more easily. We also offer to cover the tasks people would otherwise be doing, if we can. We are also about to put all papers on audio-tape for those who would find that helpful.'*

The local Talking Newspaper group has taken on the task of putting all material onto audio-tape.

Getting managers and staff on your side

Mike Leat, an advocacy worker in Surrey, describes the importance of getting support for self advocacy from managers.

> *'Before you can begin to introduce advocacy you need managerial and staff support, because both of these groups could very easily scupper any developments. I tackled this by way of staff training*

and individual discussions, literally selling the advocacy philosophy. Once you have enough people on your side, the movement takes on its own momentum. Using "quality" is a useful technique. What better test of quality is there than your customers' views! Advocacy is quite threatening, as it's shifting the balance of power from providers to users of services. Staff and managers need to be aware of this and may need support as they relinquish some of their power!'

Creating a dialogue

Mike Leat has supported the development of 'working together' meetings: 'The two service managers and the chair and secretary of the residents' committee meet together, representing their groups to share information, views and concerns, and work together on issues. These meetings will be regular and are a method by which clients' views can be represented on the management group.' Having more control over personal money was one of the first issues discussed jointly.

Networking

Building networks to share news, information and ideas supports the development of self advocacy.

The Community Living Development Team at the King's Fund Centre supports a national information exchange on self advocacy, drawing on themes and ideas from around the country.

Advocacy News contains news and letters from self advocacy groups from all over Oxfordshire. It is compiled by Jennie Ephgrave, Advocacy Development Officer, who says:

'Advocacy News speaks for itself. I do feel that this is turning into a successful venture in terms of putting people in touch with each other, highlighting issues, encouraging new self advocacy groups and creating another channel by which service users' views get through to service providers. There are certainly some strong messages in the current issue! The distribution list is growing and it is being noticed by service managers and planners.'

Training budgets

The Cell Barnes People First group has a budget of £500 to hire relevant videos or to go on courses. Other areas would like similar funding. Jennie Ephgrave, Advocacy Development Officer in Oxfordshire, says:

> *'I should like to see a training budget for service users to develop self advocacy and assertiveness skills by tapping into independently run regional or national workshops, training weekends and conferences. These normally require attendance by pairs, and are outside the remit of staff training budgets, and beyond the means of potential delegates.'*

Adults with learning difficulties as tutors

A number of courses are facilitated by adults with learning difficulties as tutors.

At **Skills for People** in Newcastle upon Tyne, all courses are planned, designed and presented by adults with learning difficulties and other disabilities. A pack is available called *Speaking Up For Yourself: How to plan and run courses that really help.* It gives practical ideas about enabling people with learning difficulties and other disabilities to design and run their own courses, and uses video and audio-tapes to complement the handbook. Careful thought has gone into making the materials clear and accessible, as the introduction explains:

> *'We have tried to avoid words that only professionals use or that might be hard to understand. We made the mistake of using the word "brainstorming" at one of our courses, and one person did not realise it just meant thinking up lots of ideas – he thought we were going to do something to his brain.'*

The WEA in Avon has employed an adult with learning difficulties to teach on its challenging behaviour course. He has successfully completed his Stage 1 FAETC City and Guilds certificate in teaching adults.

Lambeth Adult Education service employs two people with learning difficulties as advocacy tutors.

People First in London are working with four boroughs to offer training in self advocacy skills. Contracts have been devised to ensure that opportunities to progress to independent self advocacy groups are provided. The trainers planned activities together:

> *'We all sat down and thought of the most important things that people needed to learn first before they could speak up and listen to each other.'*

Chinese Whispers and role-play are among the strategies used, and rapid progress is being made: 'The eye contact and the listening skills are starting to build up after four weeks.' Declan Treanor, who advises People First in London, explains that adults with learning difficulties relate more easily to tutors who have learning difficulties: 'I've done it but I found it very difficult. People don't relate as easily to me as to people with learning difficulties.' One of the trainers with learning difficulties sees his role as preparing people for failures as well as successes: 'It's teaching people that even if they are doing everything right, we don't always get our own way.' People First (London Boroughs) have also trained staff in Haringey, and have written up the process in the paper 'Self Advocacy Awareness and User Participation Training'.

Advocacy in Action in Nottingham are known for their training on topics such as 'How to talk to top people'. Words and pictures provide cues for the trainers, who ask participants to think, for example, about what they can do when 'top people' use difficult words, interrupt or ignore them.

Courses and resources

Oxford College
Students with learning difficulties at Oxford College build confidence in speaking about themselves and learn to listen to each other during group sessions in which they follow the English

Speaking Board Syllabus. They can then take the English Speaking Board examination, which offers a recognised qualification at three levels. The course has made a positive impact, and students are now able to say what they think. They have their own committee and are represented on the Student Association Committee at the college.

Open University course P555M, Working Together

Open University *Working Together* course tutor Dorothy Atkinson says: 'Our *Working Together* course has generated much interest and activity and has made a major contribution to the development of self advocacy.' An estimated 5,000 adults with learning difficulties have studied the course in a variety of settings. Self advocacy is one of the main themes of the materials, along with others such as normalisation and independent living. Some students who have studied the course have progressed to co-tutor or facilitate study groups or to become study partners.

Students with learning difficulties joining in with regional evaluation days said what they liked about the course:

- the course design (which uses audio-tapes supported by an illustrated workbook)
- the variety and interest of the stories used
- the opportunity to work with others
- opportunities to express feelings
- talking and listening
- having choices and going in new directions
- being able to learn more.

People would like more courses, videos and conferences to follow up the course.

Jan Walmsley, one of the course team, says: '*Working Together* has given its students the chance to demonstrate that they can contribute important ideas, they too can be teachers and educators, not necessarily the eternal student.'

Staff training

Staff training is essential to underpin developments in self advocacy. The EMFEC pack *Self Advocacy at Work* involved staff and service users in the development of training materials for staff. Peter Dawson, one of the project team, commented: 'The involvement of service users in joint participation is a very powerful model of learning for the staff.' The pack is reaching a wide audience and users of the pack will be asked to evaluate it.

Training for group facilitators in South Glamorgan
The Community Education Service in South Glamorgan has recently obtained Welsh Joint Education Committee CGLI validation for its training course for facilitators of self advocacy groups. This is a 10-week introductory course designed to enable participants from a wide range of backgrounds to work with groups in a variety of settings.

The aim of the course is to ensure that prospective group facilitators have a thorough understanding of the philosophy, aims and implications of self advocacy and to enable them to recognise and develop approaches to group management and teaching and learning. The course structure provides opportunities for participants to examine their own reactions and find strategies to respond in appropriate and professional ways.

The content is based on previous courses run in South Glamorgan, originally piloted by lecturers at the Cardiff Institute of Higher Education in 1987. The course, developed as an integral part of the growth of the self advocacy movement in the county, incorporates key issues raised by the experiences of the groups.

A planning day, which was attended by self advocacy group members, parents and representatives from education, health and social services, has also helped to ensure that the course is relevant to current needs.

The course will be managed and presented by members of the recently established Community Education Disability Advisory and Resource Team (DART), supported and advised by social and health service personnel. Self advocacy group members will take part in the training both by direct input and by hosting practical placements.

Participants who successfully complete the course will be awarded the Stage One Certificate of the PGCE/Cert. Ed. (FE) qualification.

Checklists

Think about the following points and how they relate to the development of self advocacy in your area. Circle the tick according to whether each aspect is **1** – non-existent; **2** – under-developed; **3** – developed; **4** – well-developed.

	1	**2**	**3**	**4**
Control and ownership Are adults with learning difficulties controlling the development of self advocacy?	✓	✓	✓	✓
Mapping Has a survey taken place to map self advocacy groups and courses in the region or area?	✓	✓	✓	✓
Time Is there a general awareness and understanding that self advocacy takes time to set up, and more time to develop?	✓	✓	✓	✓
Transport Is transport provided for people to get to self advocacy courses, groups and conferences? Are funds available to reimburse or resource transport costs?	✓	✓	✓	✓

	1	2	3	4

Resources

Are funds available to buy in:

	1	2	3	4
– self advocacy books, materials and videos	✓	✓	✓	✓
– independent advisers	✓	✓	✓	✓
– training in self advocacy skills	✓	✓	✓	✓
– a room to meet in, preferably in a community-based setting	✓	✓	✓	✓
– secretarial support	✓	✓	✓	✓
– office costs, such as photocopying and stamps?	✓	✓	✓	✓

Training

	1	2	3	4
Is a training budget for adults with learning difficulties allocated to enable them to participate in self advocacy courses and conferences?	✓	✓	✓	✓
Are adults with learning difficulties involved in training staff?	✓	✓	✓	✓
Is a comprehensive programme of staff training and development offered in relation to self advocacy?	✓	✓	✓	✓

Courses in self advocacy

	1	2	3	4
Are courses in developing self advocacy skills widely available in your area?	✓	✓	✓	✓
Is there scope for people to progress from courses to join independent self advocacy groups?	✓	✓	✓	✓

	1	2	3	4

Adults with learning difficulties as tutors

Do adults with learning difficulties have an active role in designing and tutoring courses in self advocacy and other subjects? ✓ ✓ ✓ ✓

Are there opportunities for accreditation for adults with learning difficulties who are tutors? ✓ ✓ ✓ ✓

Equal opportunities

Do self advocacy courses and groups encourage the participation of:
- older adults ✓ ✓ ✓ ✓
- women ✓ ✓ ✓ ✓
- people from black and other ethnic minorities ✓ ✓ ✓ ✓
- people with little or no speech ✓ ✓ ✓ ✓
- people who live in rural areas ✓ ✓ ✓ ✓
- people with learning difficulties who have additional disabilities? ✓ ✓ ✓ ✓

Making information accessible

Are the following available if required:
- video equipment ✓ ✓ ✓ ✓
- taped minutes or notes ✓ ✓ ✓ ✓
- pictorial or symbol-based minutes or notes ✓ ✓ ✓ ✓
- signers for Makaton or British Sign Language ✓ ✓ ✓ ✓
- braille or Moon systems ✓ ✓ ✓ ✓
- large print for minutes ✓ ✓ ✓ ✓
- advice from speech therapists on the use of sign and symbol communication systems? ✓ ✓ ✓ ✓

	1	2	3	4

Sharing information

Are the following available in your area or region:

	1	2	3	4
– newsletters to share news and views about self advocacy	✓	✓	✓	✓
– networks of groups?	✓	✓	✓	✓

Supporting advisers and tutors

	1	2	3	4
Do people supporting self advocacy work as a team?	✓	✓	✓	✓
Do individuals working in isolation have support networks?	✓	✓	✓	✓

Relating to parents, relatives and staff

	1	2	3	4
Are parents, relatives and staff aware of the achievements and aspirations of self advocacy courses and groups?	✓	✓	✓	✓
Is there scope for a dialogue? How?	✓	✓	✓	✓

Participation

Are adults with learning difficulties involved in:

	1	2	3	4
– shortlisting and interviewing staff	✓	✓	✓	✓
– service evaluation and monitoring	✓	✓	✓	✓
– planning processes	✓	✓	✓	✓
– consultative groups and forums?	✓	✓	✓	✓

Cutting through the jargon

	1	2	3	4
Do reports, papers and meetings use clear and accessible language?	✓	✓	✓	✓

Support from the top

	1	2	3	4
Are councillors, governors and managers sympathetic to self advocacy?	✓	✓	✓	✓
Have awareness-raising sessions been held?	✓	✓	✓	✓

Resources

Materials for adults with learning difficulties to learn about self advocacy

See the Community Living Development Team listing in the address section for details of a regularly updated and complete listing.

Learning About Self Advocacy, Values Into Action, 1988.

P555(M) Working Together, Open University course available for individual, paired or group study by adults with learning difficulties. From the Open University, Walton hall, MILTON KEYNES MK7 6AA, tel: 0908 274006.

Speaking Up For Yourself: How to plan and run courses that really help, from: Skills for People, Haldane House, Tankerville Terrace, NEWCASTLE UPON TYNE NE2 3AH; tel: 091 281 8737. The following scale of charges applies to the purchase of the pack: statutory organisations £95; small voluntary organisations £50; people with or groups of people with disabilities £20; plus £2 postage and packing in all cases.

Self Advocacy at Work is available at £35.00, plus £5.00 postage and packing, from: EMFEC, Robins Wood House, Robins Wood Road, Aspley, NOTTINGHAM NG8 3NH.

Suggested reading

P. Allen and C. Scales *Residents' Rights: Helping people with learning difficulties understand their housing rights.* Pavilion Publishing, 1990.

Mariette Clare *Developing Self Advocacy Skills.* Further Education Unit/REPLAN, 1990.

Steve Dowson *Keeping It Safe*. Values Into Action, 1990.

Simon Gardner, Gary Bourlet and Annette McDonald *Self Advocacy Awareness and User Participation Training*. People First, 1992.

John Hersov and Deborah Cooper *We Can Change the Future*. Skill: The National Bureau for Students with Disabilities, 1986.

People First Newsletter. Available quarterly by subscription.

Ken Simons *Sticking Up For Yourself: The experiences of people involved in self-advocacy by people with learning difficulties. The Bristol Advocacy Project*. Joseph Rowntree Foundation, 1993.

Jeannie Sutcliffe *Adults with Learning Difficulties: Education for choice and empowerment*. NIACE in association with the Open University Press, 1990.

Talking Together. Views of people with learning difficulties and their carers on future services. Bridges (formerly APMH), 1991.

Andrea Whittaker *Supporting Self Advocacy*. King's Fund Centre, 1991.

Paul Williams and Bonnie Shoultz *We Can Speak for Ourselves*. Souvenir Press, 1982, re-issued 1991.

Useful addresses

A full and regularly updated listing of resources to support self advocacy is available from the Community Living Development Team at the King's Fund Centre. Conferences on self advocacy are also hosted by the team from time to time, while an information exchange newsletter on self advocacy is produced regularly.

Advocacy in Action
Princes House
32 Park Row
NOTTINGHAM NG1 6GR
Tel: 0602 500537/500631

Community Living Development Team
King's Fund Centre
126 Albert Street
LONDON NW1 7NF
Tel: 071 267 6111

The Examinations Secretary
English Speaking Board (International) Ltd
26a Princes Street
Southport PR8 1EQ
Tel: 0704 501730

Further Education Unit
Spring Gardens
Citadel Place
Tinworth Street
LONDON SE11 5EH
Tel: 071 962 1280

John Hersov
(Independent self advocacy consultant)
23 Willoughby Road
Hampstead
LONDON NW3 1RT
Tel: 071 794 7162

National Citizen Advocacy Resource and Advisory Centre
Unit 2K, Leroy House
436 Essex Road
LONDON N1 3QP
Tel: 071 359 8289

National Institute of Adult Continuing Education
Continuing Education for Adults with Learning Difficulties
Charles Street Adult Education Centre
Charles Street
LUTON LU2 0EB
Tel: 0582 22566

People First
Instrument House
207–215 King's Cross Road
LONDON WC1X 7DB
Tel: 071 713 6400

The Joseph Rowntree Foundation
c/o Dr Linda Ward
Programme Adviser (Disability)
Norah Fry Research Centre
32 Tyndalls Park Road
BRISTOL BS8 1PY
Tel: 0272 238137

Skill: National Bureau for Students with Disabilities
366 Brixton Road
LONDON SW9 7AA
Tel: 071 274 0565

Skills for People
Haldane House
Tankerville Terrace
NEWCASTLE UPON TYNE NE2 3AH
Tel: 091 281 8737

Values Into Action
Oxford House
Derbyshire Street
LONDON E2 6HG
Tel: 071 729 5436

Notes

Notes